THE *Lazy* MILLIONAIRE

Frederick Fell Publishers, Inc
2131 Hollywood Blvd., Suite 305
Hollywood, Fl 33020
www.Fellpub.com
email: Fellpub@aol.com

Frederick Fell Publishers, Inc
2131 Hollywood Blvd., Suite 305
Hollywood, Fl 33020

Copyright © 2008 by Marc Fisher. All rights reserved.

All rights reserved, including the right to reproduce this book or portions thereof in any form whatsoever, For information address to Frederick Fell Subsidiary Rights Department, 2131 Hollywood Boulevard, Suite 305, Hollywood, Florida 33020.

First Frederick Fell trade book edition September 2008

For information about special discounts for bulk purchases, Please contact Frederick Fell Special Sales at business@fellpublishers.com.

Designed by Elena Solis

Manufactured in the United States of America

10 9 8 7 6 5 4 3 2 1

Library of Congress Cataloging-in-Publication Data

Fisher, Marc, 1953-
 The lazy millionaire / Marc Fischer.
    p. cm.
 ISBN 0-88391-165-5 (pbk. : alk. paper)
 1. Success in business. 2. Millionaires. 3. Wealth. 4. Success--Psychological aspects.
I. Title.
 HF5386.F41556 2008
 650.1--dc22

                    2008023697

ISBN-13   978-0-88391-165-5
ISBN-10   0-88391-165-5

MARC FISHER

THE

Lazy
MILLIONAIRE

"Geniuses Often Accomplish More
When They Work Less."
—Leonardo Da Vinci

BIOGRAPHY

MARC FISHER: Born in Montreal, Canada, in 1953, Marc Fisher studied philosophy, literature and worked several years in the publishing business.

His first success came in 1987 with THE INSTANT MILLIONAIRE, (New World Library) a short philosophical fable. The book sold 2 million copies around the world, and has been published in more then 30 countries (including Japan, Germany, Russia, U.K., China, Sweden, Norway, Greece, Italy, Spain, Korea...)

Author of THE MILLIONAIRE'S SECRETS (Simon and Schuster) THE GOLFER AND THE MILLIONAIRE (Prima Publishing), Marc Fisher also penned several psychological thrillers.

Avid golfer, he also likes jogging, yoga and travels regularly in Europe. He lives in Montreal, Canada, with his wife Deborah and daughter Julia.

"Geniuses often accomplish more when they work less"
—Leonardo daVinci

DEDICATION

To my partner in good and… extremely good times: Deborah

TABLE OF CONTENTS

PART I

CH1   What is a lazy millionaire?.. 15

CH2   Why aren't you already a lazy millionaire?................................... 19

CH3   The lazy millionaire loves work…particularly when his assets do all the hard work!.. 21

CH4   The lazy millionaire grows rich quicker thanks to his mentor........ 27

CH5   The lazy millionaire lets his objective work for him...................... 33

CH6   The lazy millionaire preserves his sanity by following the Principle of Least Effort.. 39

CH7   The lazy millionaire plays according to Parkinson's Law............... 45

CH8   The lazy millionaire loves work … that of others!......................... 51

CH9   The lazy millionaire is positive... 55

CH10   The lazy millionaire tackles the most profitable tasks first............. 61

CH11   The lazy millionaire always strives to pay the lowest price............ 69

CH12   The lazy millionaire tracks minor, invisible expenses.................... 77

CH13   The lazy millionaire saves without suffering................................. 81

CH14   The lazy millionaire lives like a king on a beggar's salary!............. 91

CH15   The lazy millionaire trusts his intuition.. 95

CH16   Give yourself the lazy millionaire's agenda!................................. 101

PART II

THE ART OF ALWAYS BEING ON VACATION

CH1   Take your time, because...It's your time!...........................107
CH2   Free yourself from the tyranny of work!........................113
CH3   Don't buy until you decide to buy...................................119
CH4   Free yourself from false obligations.............................127
CH5   Write: "Do nothing!"In your agenda... 133
CH6   Are you afraid to stop?..141
CH7   To get there on time, leave...early!................................145
CH8   Why I shave in my car...151
CH9   Do you spend your time...vacuuming?...........................155
CH10 The ultimate secret to making the most of your time......159

XI

PART I

❧CHAPTER 1

WHAT IS A LAZY MILLIONAIRE?

"There are only four types of officer: First, there are the lazy, stupid ones. Leave them alone, they do no harm.

Second, there are the hard-working intelligent ones. They make excellent staff officers, ensuring that every detail is properly considered.

Third, there are the hard-working, stupid ones. These people are a menace and must be fired at once.

Finally, there are the intelligent lazy ones. They are suited for the highest office."

These wise and humorous thoughts, written by General von Manstein about the German army, hit me like a ton of bricks when I first read them.

Because ever since I was young, I was taught the virtue of hard work.

Because ever since I was young, —and throughout my adult life —I was told over and over again that lazy people are good for nothing. In some cases this is actually true.

But what about you?

You have probably also been told until you were sick of hearing it that nothing in life comes easily, "no pain no gain", and frustration and sacrifices are par for the course.

Of course, a lot of hard-working people do become millionaires.

The fact is: by the time those people have achieved financial independence they are generally so old, that they are unable to really enjoy the fruit of their labor during retirement.

What's worse is that they have sacrificed almost EVERYTHING to achieve their goal: their family, their free time, and very often their health.

Is it worth it?

NO!

At least in the eyes of the Lazy Millionaire.

The Lazy Millionaire wants to become financially independent, but he does not want to stop living for 30 or 40 years in order to achieve this goal.

This is what sets him apart, not only from most people, but also from regular millionaires.

Take John Paul Getty, as an example.

In his time, he was the richest man in the world. However, in How to be rich, one of his autobiographical works, he confessed that in spite of his millions, he was never able to take more than seven consecutive days of vacation, and that even when he was on vacation, he was never able to go an entire day without receiving or making several telephone calls in order to resolve various urgent problems!

What's the point of being a millionaire (or a billionaire, in Getty's case) if you can't spend a single day without being inundated with problems?

I'd rather be a lazy millionaire!

But first, just so that things are perfectly clear, let me explain what I mean by the term "lazy millionaire".

It's simple: a lazy millionaire is someone who has acquired a significant fortune of between \$1 million and \$10 million quickly and relatively easily.

Why between \$1 million and \$10 million?

The lower number is easy to understand, of course. You can't be considered a millionaire unless you have at least... \$1 million!

The upper limit requires some explanation.

I set the upper limit at \$10 million because, among all of the millionaires in America, 95% have a fortune of between \$1 million and \$10 million. For the most part, they are regular people like you and me; people who rarely make the headlines...

I must specify that, even though I set the lower limit at \$1 million, with today's interest rates and the ever increasing cost of living, having

16

$1 million in the bank by the age of 40 will not provide a very exciting lifestyle without touching the principle.

And once you start to reduce your principle, you will not be able to enjoy the life of a lazy millionaire for very long.

Today, you need $3 or $4 million in order to live the life of a lazy millionaire.

If you manage to accumulate $10 million, which is very doable if you already have $2 million or $3 million by the age of 50 or 55, and if you live 25 or 30 more years, which is the average lifespan these days, you will most definitely enjoy a much more comfortable life …

If you want to accumulate a significantly greater fortune ($50 million, $250 million, or more) you would have to give up the mentality, habits, and comfort level of a lazy millionaire.

~~~So what else is a lazy millionaire?

A lazy millionaire doesn't need a university degree, or an exceptional talent, to make it.

Unlike rich heirs, or those who have received a small (or large!) cash injection from their parents, a lazy millionaire doesn't need more than one generation to become wealthy.

He doesn't need 50 years, or even 30 years…

He becomes independently wealthy in less than 20 years, which means that if he starts early (which is an exception), at age 20, or even 40, he will die of laughter, and not of exhaustion like his peers!

The Lazy Millionaire can be successful in achieving his goal, possibly, in 10 years. He may even do this in 5 years, even though this would indeed be quite an achievement, and is rare.

Looking at the path travelled in such a short time, and at his bank account, the Lazy Millionaire is often amazed that the task that he accomplished was so easy.

The Lazy Millionaire has a way of thinking, of spending and of using his time that is completely different from ordinary people.

And this is why he is a lazy millionaire!!

But what exactly is the difference between a lazy millionaire and you —and why aren't you already one?

✂CHAPTER 2

WHY AREN'T YOU ALREADY A LAZY MILLIONAIRE?

What is the one fundamental difference between a lazy millionaire and you?

It's easy: you HAVE to work 8, 10, or 12 hours per day; 5, 6, or 7 days per week; 48, 50, or 52 weeks per year!

The Lazy Millionaire… DOESN'T!

But why do you spend so many hours working?

For one of these 12 reasons:

1. The reason that comes to mind most spontaneously is that you are underpaid for the work you do. Yes, you are U-N-D-E-R-P-A-I-D because you are not sufficiently aware of your real value. You agree to work for $8, $15, or $75 per hour when you could be earning $200, $500, or $1,000! Yes, $1,000 per hour without having to be a lawyer or a plastic surgeon!

2. You manage your time ineffectively, and spend too much time doing what you do. You spend your time confusing urgent matters with important matters, and more importantly, you spend most of your time on tasks that pay very little, because you don't follow the Principle of Least Effort, or the 80/20 rule (i.e. the Pareto principle), which could help you to double or even quintuple your income…

3. You don't realize that small and frequent invisible expenses have a huge negative financial effect on your life. More to the point: you live beyond your means, which means that you have to work more than ever without stopping, and without ever being able to invest anything or put any money aside…

4. You always pay the full price when you make purchases, when you should be paying the price of the lazy millionaire, and thereby saving thousands of dollars … (for example: $2,800 on a brand new car!)

5. You haven't grasped the amazing virtue of (early) saving… and

never figured out how the money used for a daily pack of cigarettes could be used to build a real fortune...

6.   You are the exact opposite of the lazy millionaire: you are a conscientious slave! You are a worrier or a perfectionist who is incapable of delegating and having others do the work for you...

7.   You have no sources of alternative revenue, especially residual which would free you from the obligation of working many hours each day until the age of retirement, or even longer, because you are aren't able to maintain your comfort level without your salary...

8.   You aren't using the powerful secret of the objective to your advantage, which could enable you, for example, to earn $15,000 more in just two hours, year after year or get your hands on your first million in three years. (Or you are using the power of the objective, but in a pernicious way, without even realizing it, and you are losing thousands of dollars per year as a result!)

9.   You rarely use the leverage effect, while the lazy millionaire uses it systematically.

10. YOU don't have a fiscal structure that enables you to reap all of the possible legal benefits of your revenues. In short, you mimic the vast majority of people, who work from January to May just to pay their taxes and benefits!

11. You are unaware of benefits of the invisible "Bucket and spade" technique in your relationships with others: colleagues, employees, family —and you may be less positive than you think you are...

12. Finally, and more generally speaking, you went to school but you did not receive the education of a lazy millionaire so you are convinced that lazy millionaires do not deserve to earn so much money, because they only work half or one-tenth as much as you!

You are convinced that they are even less deserving of driving a car that is nicer than yours, or having a nicer house (not to mention their cottage or ocean side condo!), or taking vacations so often to the most exotic places that you will spend your entire life only dreaming about!

✂CHAPTER 3

THE LAZY MILLIONAIRE LOVES THE WORK…
PARTICULARLY WHEN HIS ASSETS DO ALL THE HARD WORK

A few years ago, I drove home from the dealer at the wheel of a two-year-old BMW 525. It was in excellent condition. I had wanted to buy it with an unexpected check I received from the publisher.

I excitedly showed it to my wife, who was "busy" watering the flowers.

Instead of congratulating me on my new acquisition, as I had hoped she would do, she frowned and asked me flatly:

"You bought yourself a new car?"

"Uh, no… I put down a $200 deposit to hold it. I wanted to show it to you before I bought it…"

"We already have a BMW! Why buy another one? And we have a mini-van. We don't need three cars!"

"Exactly. The guy is prepared to give me $10,000 for our old BMW, and I convinced him to lower his price by $8,000. He's almost giving it to me! I'm getting a $48,000 car for $30,000.

I stood proud of my clever answer.
"Not $30,000," my wife correctly observed, as she explained: "$40,000, because, in exchange, you're giving him a car that's worth $10,000."

Now, if you're anything like me, you hate it when your wife contradicts you.

Especially when she's right!

I quickly went on the offensive. "True, but it's an opportunity that doesn't come along very often, and our BMW is already five years old, and is beginning to look tired, don't you think?"

My wife remained stony faced: "What I think is that you should buy that little white house I showed you the other day instead."

To make a long story short, we went to visit the little white house that very night, at the wheel of... my old beamer, because I had given the key to "my" shiny new car back to the seller, who was kind enough to return my $200 deposit.

The house wasn't much to look at, and the price the seller was asking seemed a little excessive: $125,000 (A price that's unheard of these days —I know!). His daughter, who had lived there for years, didn't want to leave, which was making it even harder to sell, considering that most people buy a house so they can live in it.

I thought about it for a while. I could use this situation to my own advantage since I did not intend to live there, of course. So I made a fairly low offer of $75,000, BUT I assured the owner that I was willing to sign a 3-year lease with his daughter without increasing her rent.

The seller, who had owned the house for 20 years, made me a surprising counter-offer of $82,000 (I found out why later!), which I accepted without further negotiations. I did not want to push my luck any further!!!

I then realized I had bought a house instead of a new car (well, almost new)...

A house that would generate small monthly revenue. After taxes, which were low, the mortgage and insurance, it left me with $300 every month.

"You see," my wife said, "this is much better than making car payments of $300 per month. It gives a differential of $600 per month."

"But I was going to pay cash for the car!"

"I know, but what I mean is that IF you were to make a $300 payment, you would have a differential of $600."

She had contradicted me again.

And she was right yet again.

And I was annoyed again.

But deep down, I secretly congratulated myself for having chosen this woman —assuming of course that it was me who chose her and not the other way around, because generally speaking, it's the woman who chooses the man, even though the man may think differently!

Yes, I patted myself on the back once again for allowing myself to be chosen by this woman, who in addition to being extremely beautiful, knew how to handle money and wasn't a big spender, unlike the wives of some of my friends. How do they survive?

If you are unclear on the concept, a differential is not just a part of the car that... well, I don't really know what it does!

In financial jargon, a differential means the following:

If you use your money to earn $300 instead of spending $300, you add these two amounts together to determine the real impact of your actions on your bank account: the sum ($600) is known as the differential.

Here is another equally interesting example of a differential.

We have a tiny cottage that, for various reasons (maybe because we have a swimming pool and a yard at home), we don't even use three times per year. Despite its small size, it generates a few expenses, including heat, electricity, a total of around $200 per month.

The other day, my wife suggested that we should rent it out, because we never use it.

She told me: "If we were to rent it out for $500 per month, that would represent a differential of $700."

She was right again.

Because the tenant would pay for the heating and electricity. Instead of a $200 monthly expense, I would have a $500 monthly revenue.

**People often forget the concept of differential.
Lazy millionaires never forget it.**

And if they do forget, their wives don't!

Especially if they are anything like my wife!

That's why, every time he gets the chance, as soon as possible and as often as possible, the lazy millionaire tries to use his money (or the bank's money!) to acquire assets instead of creating liabilities!

For those who are not yet familiar with this jargon, let's just say that if you buy a car, and out of necessity you do not pay cash but commit to making payments for 3 or 4 or 5 years, you have created a liability.

I know that a bank will include your car in your list of assets on your balance sheet, especially if it is paid for in whole, but your car loses 20% of its value during the first year, and is a source of expenses (monthly payments, often at very high interest rates, insurance, repairs, gas, etc.). I know you need a car: it's very difficult to travel the streets at the wheel of a… duplex!

But who says you need a new car every two or three years? What is wrong with your five or seven year-old car? Except the fact that your neighbor changes his every three years? Put aside vanity and start using your money the lazy millionaire way! When you are starting out, keep your old car, which is what I did.

What's more, by putting off the need to buy a new car, you do not reduce your borrowing capacity, which is based on all of your monthly obligations. Your "ratio" will improve immediately. The bank will like it. And so will you.

Instead of buying a car, if you buy a (good!) property that you rent out (good!), it constitutes an asset because, in principle, it gains in value every year and generates passive revenue every month, in the sense that you don't need to be there and work in order to accumulate it.

This is the basic definition of passive revenue, with the extreme example obviously being interest revenue generated by a bank deposit...

But passive income is not always as "passive" as we wished in the first place. I soon found out at my expense.

Indeed, one month after I purchased the little white house, it became clear to me why the seller had let it go for peanuts: his daughter probably never paid the rent.

At any rate, she only paid for the first month.

At the beginning, my optimism as a young investor was challenged.

But I immediately told myself: "That's a sign life is sending you to help you make more money. Instead of keeping the house, sell it!"

When the tenant was two months late, I offered to cancel her debt and give her another $500 to move out immediately. I did this on the advice of my real estate mentor.

He knew I got the amazing deal only because I accepted to keep the owner's daughter as a long-term tenant...

But now she was not paying the rent so I did not have to keep my promise.

Anyway, the tenant accepted my proposal and left the next week. Once I paid the commission, I was left with a profit of around $30,000.

Since I paid $82,000 for the house, it was $42,000 more than I paid.

Once I paid the commission, I was left with $50,000, or a profit of around $30,000.

With my initial $30,000, I now had the $60,000,and thanks to a few (free!) financing tips from my mentor I bought three other houses, which I refinanced instead of reselling.

Six years later, I owned a nice real estate portfolio that was evaluated by the bank (which means a conservative estimate) at $3,000,000...

Yes, $3 million...

I had taken the $30,000 that I planned to spend on a car and transformed it into assets of $3 million,

Yes, I bought a frightful little house instead of a car: I bought an ASSET instead of a LIABILITY.

An asset that, during the first year, and still assuming a 5% annual increase, (the average over the past 50 years) would make me $150,000 richer…

I'm not saying this to blow my own trumpet…

Because for people who are truly "wealthy", an asset (whether in real estate or otherwise) that is worth $3 million is "peanuts".

I just wanted to show you how someone who knew absolutely nothing about the real estate market (although I had a wonderful mentor), and who was also a… writer, was able to transform $30,000 into $3 million in only 6 years…

On top of that, these properties would generate $50,000 of passive income per year for me, in exchange for 5 or 6 hours of work per week, on average!

I say on average, because sometimes I do nothing for 3 weeks, and I don't even hear from my tenants, which gives me the impression that I am being… paid to do nothing!

That's the real beauty of passive revenue, and it is precisely for this reason that it is something that lazy millionaires really like!

I know that $50,000 isn't the be all and end all…

But many people have to make do with far less in retirement…

So when he time comes for me to retire (whatever that might mean for a novelist), I will gradually sell off these houses, which will be completely paid off, and which will probably be worth twice or three times as much, so maybe $10 million!

Yes, I know, some of the money will go to taxes, but I will still have some left over, won't I?

At any rate, more than the old age pension that the government will pay out… if it is still paying it at all!

When I tell people about this adventure, they often ask me the following questions:

Has it prevented me from writing?

No. I wrote my yearly book.

Do I have more worries, now, with all these properties?

Yes, I'll admit to that. But as they say, you get out of things what you put into them.

Did I have to work harder?

Yes, I have sacrificed several weekends on renovations that I've had carried out but have had to supervise, and I have played golf less often than I would have liked...

Do we go without?

No. We have maintained the same quality of life.

Am I happy to have made these sacrifices?

YES.

VERY.

Because in all honesty, I've enjoyed it, and it has taken my mind off my work as a writer.

Every time we bought a new house, my wife said something like:

"The rent from this one will pay our electricity bills."

Or: "The rent from this one will pay our taxes!"

Or even: "The rent from this one will pay for our daughter's daycare!"

Then I realize something:

At the moment when your passive revenue exceeds your expenses... YOU ARE FREE!

Yes, FREE!

Think about it for a while.

What it means is: you do not have to have millions in your bank account to be financially independent.

You just have to have a passive income that exceed you expenses.

Isn't that great?

Okay, I hear you saying: it's fine to buy houses and have passive revenue and assets that increase in value over time, but I don't have the $30,000 I need to get started, so what can I do?

Well, then, you begin searching immediately for the person I'll be talking about in the next chapter!

CHAPTER 4

THE LAZY MILLIONAIRE GETS RICHER QUICKER THANKS TO HIS MENTOR

Newton said: "If I have seen further, it is by standing on the shoulders of giants…"

He was obviously talking about past giants, referring to the philosophers and wise men who came before him, and whose works he had studied.

The lazy millionaire does the same thing.

He stands on the shoulders of giants.

He lets the great men "carry" him…

Instead of saying, like everyone else, "We always need someone smaller than us", he wisely says "We always need someone bigger than us!"

It's less work, and it enables us to take… giant steps!

That's exactly what the Lazy Millionaire wants. In fact, IT IS his specialty!

He draws inspiration from the example set by those who came before him and who accomplished great things.

Plato had Socrates as a professor.

Alexander the Great had Aristotle.

A little closer to our time, Steven Spielberg had Hollywood icon Lou Wasserman as a mentor.

Donald Trump had his father as a mentor. He was a real estate developer in the Bronx, and young Donald followed him to work sites.

Warren Buffett, whose fortune is evaluated at $40 billion, had Benjamin Graham as a mentor. At the end of his high school studies, he accidentally came across his book, *The Intelligent Investor*, which has remained a classic.

Fascinated by this work, the young Buffett decided to register for a course that Graham was giving at Columbia University.

After earning his Master's degree in Economics, and after being told no for three years, (even if he was offering his services for free!) Buffett landed a job at the company run by Graham. He worked for two years under his supervision then decided to start out on his own. He did for himself what he was doing for his mentor. Five years later, at the age of thirty, Buffett was a millionaire. The rest is history.

This is the amazing power of a mentor.

Why take years and lose thousand of dollars learning the hard way when you can learn from the best if you are smart (and lazy!) enough to find the right mentor?

In his book called *Ogilvy on Advertising*, advertising icon David Ogilvy relates an enlightening anecdote. He was talking with Stanley Resor, who headed the famous J. Walter Thompson advertising agency for 45 years: "Every year," Resor told him in confidence, "we spend hundreds of millions of dollars of our clients' money. And what do we learn from it? Nothing. Two years ago, I asked four of our employees to attempt to identify the factors that usually work. They identified 12!"

David Ogilvy commented:

"I was too polite to tell him that I knew 96!"

Just imagine the immense benefit that the young cub in advertising could have drawn from having David Ogilvy as a mentor!

How many years did it take him to learn how to use these 96 factors to his advantage?

How much money had he spent —his clients' money of course, but his own as well —to acquire this priceless experience?

I have a friend who is a real estate investor. He isn't the biggest, but he isn't the smallest either, with 300 doors, worth several million dollars, because he was intelligent enough to invest when he was very young. In fact, he was so intelligent that he got his hand on buildings for $150,000 that today are worth $700,000 or $800,000...

One day at lunchtime, I asked him how he had come to the decision to buy a certain building. "It's easy. I have 37 criteria!"

What a gold mine these 37 criteria could end up being for the young man who succeeds in making my friend his mentor!

In fact, a mentor is of inestimable value.

The lazy millionaire knows it.

He will try, from the very start of his career, to find one.

He will not hesitate to dedicate his time to this task. A great deal of time.

Because the mentor who is worthy of this name knows how to:

1.   accelerate his learning process in an extraordinary manner, by sharing the fruits of his experience.

2.   save him from a lot costly mistakes, although not all of them, because the young protégé will not "understand" all of the secrets that his mentor tells him, even though the mentor may have explained them fully. There are some things one can only understand by experiencing them for ourselves. And while the mentor knows a lot, he might not know everything. Especially the way the modern world is changing at an incredibly fast pace. If, at the end of his life, Henry Ford had repeated to a young protégé that the only cars that sold were black cars, he would have been giving him bad advice!

3.   open doors for him and put him into contact with influential people, and giving him his first chance by hiring him or asking a friend or business contact to hire him.

4.   offer him financial assistance for a project by lending him money (e.g.: $30,000 to buy his first home!), (or) introducing him to his bank manager, or co-signing a loan. (for him)

5.   more generally speaking and equally important, influence him positively through his own experience, philosophy on life, and style...
But how can you find a mentor?

Here are a few rules and tips:

1.   Mentors, even retired ones, are generally busy people, whose time is valuable. Never abuse their time, and understand that it is possible they will not be able to arrange a meeting with you for a few weeks, or even months, especially if they are still active and they travel a lot. Be patient. And confident. If they can't meet (with) you immediately, this doesn't mean that they don't want to meet with you —it usually means that they simply aren't available.

2.   Be daring and creative in the way you approach them, and introduce yourself. Remember the film *The Six Degrees of Separation*, which claims that ONLY six people separate us all from any person in the world. I don't know if this principle means that I will meet Bill Gates, Steven Spielberg, or the Pope one day, but there is some truth to this principle. You undoubtedly know someone who knows someone who knows ... the mentor that you would like to meet!

3.   Although they are very busy, mentors are often more available than we think. And more importantly, in your quest for a mentor, don't believe that it is an impossible mission, because then it risks… becoming one!

4.   Before meeting with your mentor, read Dale Carnegie's book *How to Make Friends and Influence people*. This book will teach you (or remind you) of the basic principle of human psychology: in order to arouse someone's interest or get something from him, what you must do is show him how he will benefit if… he gives you what you want! Of course, given the obvious disproportion that exists between you and your mentor, this principle doesn't always apply perfectly, because your mentor will not necessarily think that you have anything to offer him. But keep this principle in mind anyway when you meet him, and when you meet anyone you want something from, like a job, a service, a loan… For example, offer your services, even free of charge, like the young Warren Buffet did. He didn't fare too badly, did he? Make sure your future mentor knows how important it is for you to work with him, or simply to become his protégé

5.   Do your homework before you meet with your mentor. Try to learn as much as possible about him: about his start, about his career, his achievements, his dreams, his charitable and social endeavours, his hobbies and his passions. Speak to him about these things during your meeting, and remind him of his most illustrious ventures. Ask him for details or simply ask him to tell you again. I have never met anyone who didn't love to recount the story of their brilliant and modest beginnings, even when they have already told the story 100 times! Flatter him. But do it intelligently. I don't know very many people who do not react to compliments. Even God is touched, I believe, when we praise Him. There must be a reason, right?

6.   Be brief and polite in all contacts with your mentor. Listen attentively —and religiously! Let him tell you everything he has to say, without interrupting him. Thank him for giving you a few minutes of his precious time.

And make sure his advice and the example he gives you are not in vain: put them into practice that same day!

Not in a month or a week: immediately!

"If you don't do it right away, you'll never do it!"

That's what all lazy millionaires do, and that's why they take giant steps when the people around them, who are often more educated, more intelligent, and harder working, find themselves running around in circles for their entire lives!

Lazy millionaires also do something that a lot of people do not do.

They use a really simple secret —an extraordinary lever that literally makes their revenue explode, and makes it possible for them to earn 2, 5, 10, or even 100 times more money without having to work harder...

Do you like what I am saying?

Read on!

✂CHAPTER 5

THE LAZY MILLIONAIRE
LETS HIS OBJECTIVE WORK FOR HIM

One day, legendary golf champion Ben Hogan played a round of golf at the Los Angeles Country Club.

Hole No. 5 (on the North Course) is a 476-yard par-5 with a green that is not visible from the tee because of the waviness of the fairway.

There is a row of four large palm trees behind the green. When Ben Hogan stood at the tee, he immediately asked his caddy to give him a target, because the green was not visible, and Hogan was playing there for the first time.

His caddy recommended that he aim for the palm trees.

"Which one?" replied Ben Hogan, to his caddy's amazement.

And probably to your amazement too, even if you are a golfer…

I found this anecdote in the wonderful book *Golf is Not a Game of Perfect*, written by sports psychologist Bob Rotella who, over the course of his prestigious career, has been personal advisor to such talented golfers as Tom Kite, Nick Price, Curtis Strange, Brad Faxon, and Davis Love...

Here is how he explained the somewhat strange question asked by Ben Hogan: "This story is cited sometimes as an example of Hogan's perfectionism. But what it really suggests is Hogan's knowledge of one of the fundamental psychological principles in golf:

« BEFORE TAKING ANY SHOT, A GOLFER MUST PICK OUT THE SMALLEST POSSIBLE TARGET.»

Rotella continues:

«This may seem obvious to some people. But the number of golfers who don't do it continually amazes me. When I'm at a clinic or pro-am tournament with someone who's just sprayed his ball into the next country, I sometimes ask what he was aiming at when he hit the errant shot. Usually, the reply is something like, "I was aiming down the left side." Or "down the middle". Or people might say, "I don't know what I was aiming at. I just knew I didn't want to miss left. That's not good enough. Aiming down the middle is the equivalent of trying to go to Los Angeles by flying to an airport somewhere in California!»

He adds:

« The brain and nervous system respond best when the eyes focus on the smallest possible target. Why this is so is not important. It just happens to be the way the human system works.»

When I read these lines, I couldn't help but be struck by the similarity between the way these golfers act and the way some people with whom I interact at my conferences or during private consultations act (or think!).

In fact, I cannot count the number of people whom I have asked to tell me their financial objective for the year, and who have replied:

1. that they do not have one;
2. that their objective is to pay off their debts;
3. that their objective is to find a more lucrative job;
4. that they want to make a fortune.

These objectives all have the same defect: they are too VAGUE!

With money, the equivalent of the smallest target possible is definitely not a minuscule monetary objective, which could be depressing, but:

THE MOST ACCURATE OBJECTIVE POSSIBLE.

And what is the most accurate objective possible?

It is an objective that has AN AMOUNT AND A TIMELINE FOR ACHIEVING IT.

One day at a conference, during the break, an excited young woman came up to me and said: "Mr. Fisher! Mr. Fisher! I have to tell you something! Last week, I had a job interview. I was telling myself: '"$25,000 . . . $25,000! I won't accept anything less than $25,000!' But the day before the interview, I came across your book *The Instant Millionaire* in a bookstore. I read it in one sitting, and then I told myself: '$40,000 . . . $40,000! I won't accept anything less!' And do you know what? I got it!

I warmly congratulated her, and said: "Not bad for two hours of reading!"

Not bad at all indeed...

$15,000 more...

How much is that per hour?

It's $7,500 per hour!

And she would have this extra $15,000 YEAR AFTER YEAR…

Not only would she have it year after year, but her eventual salary increases would be based on a $40,000 starting salary, and not on the $25,000 that she was originally expecting...

And if she changed jobs, she would be able to say that she had previously been earning $40,000, which would immediately place her in a better category than if she had accepted a job at $25,000…

If she had followed the philosophy of the intelligent worker instead of the lazy worker, how many years would it have taken her to increase from $25,000 to $40,000, assuming a hypothetical annual increase of 5%?

I'll leave that one for you to calculate —It tires me out just thinking about it!

In fact, without even knowing it, after she read *The Instant Millionaire*, this young woman started to think like a lazy millionaire...

All she had done (and it doesn't have to he complicated to be effective…) was allow her objective to do the work for her!

How many people do exactly the opposite?

Instead of letting their objective work for them… they WORK!

Like madmen.

Yes! They work, and work, and work… for next to nothing!

Like those golfers whose balls fly all over the place—and rarely where they want them to go!—their objective is neither specific enough nor lofty enough.

They seem to be running in place, despite their perseverance and intelligence, and the overtime hours that they accumulate, to the point of making themselves ill or so nervous and irritable that nobody —not even their loved ones —dares approach them!

The most amazing example of the power of the objective I ever witnessed was when I was working in the publishing division of Quebecor, a media oriented Canadian company. It's founder, Pierre Péladeau, was a brilliant businessman who'd started with $1500 borrowed from his mom and went one to build a 10 billion dollar empire.

In 1982, the company was doing well, but Péladeau was not satisfied. He had a dream. He wanted to gross one billion a year. He said he liked the figure.

One fall morning in 1982, in the modest offices that he occupied at the time on Roy St. in Montréal, the colourful entrepreneur called together his vice-presidents, and stunned them by announcing that he wanted to increase sales to $1 billion in ten years...

And how did he plan to achieve this amazing objective?

Quite simple: by making one acquisition per month!

Yes, one acquisition —buying out one existing company each month!

It was extremely ambitious, and virtually inconceivable —in fact, it was a statement that was so over-the-top that several vice-presidents left the meeting with their faces ashen, their eyebrows arched, and their scepticism deeper than ever.

It did not take Pierre Péladeau ten years to achieve the $1 billion mark.

See what happened.

In 1982, Quebecor's sales were $208 million.

In 1983, sales increased to $221 million, which represents a modest leap of $13 million.

In 1984, sales reached $279 million, which represents a juicy increase of more than 25%!

In 1985, sales increased to $342 million, for another solid 22% increase...

In 1986, sales grew soundly to reach $446 million, yes, nearly half a billion dollars!

And that's when the real explosion happened, making the company's growth curve resemble a geometric progression, which we all know constantly doubles the previous number in a series...

In 1987, Quebecor's sales were $650 million...

Finally, in 1988, sales virtually doubled, breaking the $1 billion mark, soaring to $1.284 billion!

And he did that in only six years!

Not ten, only six!

Did he work harder?

No, he continued working the same hours, which were in fact already long hours. (He was more of a workaholic then a lazy millionaire!) So he could not really work a lot more.

But his objective could.

Of course, you wont necessarily reach your objectives simply because you set your sights on a specific amount and deadline.

But —and this is the really important point:

YOU WILL NEARLY ALWAYS ACHIEVE BETTER RESULTS WITH AN OBJECTIVE, THAN WITHOUT.

And the thing is, you won't necessarily work harder.

This is why setting an objective is so precious to the Lazy Millionaire.

A lazy millionaire knows that the size of a fish is determined by... the size of the aquarium!

For the Lazy Millionaire, the equation for fortune and success is simple.

Since: AQUARIUM = OBJECTIVE
Therefore LARGER OBJECTIVE = LARGER SUCCESS

Of course, if you are fine with the idea of your little fish (read: income) staying little, then let them spend their whole life in the same small aquarium!

That is what bosses sometimes do with their employees.

Husbands sometimes do this with their wives —or vice versa.

And parents sometimes do it with their children.

Especially fathers, who can't stand it when their sons earn more than they do...

Sometimes the sons themselves decide, either consciously or otherwise, to stay in the same aquarium as their fathers, for fear of upsetting them and humiliating them with their overwhelming success, because they must follow the "order" that, without even knowing it, was dictated to them when they were children, and because they were good children, they were "obedient". We are all familiar with the outcome.

In your own life as you know it, haven't YOU also been content to swim in an aquarium that is far too small for YOU?

We just saw how the lazy millionaire wisely —and effortlessly —increases the size of his income thanks to the magical lever of the objective...

However, he does not only want to earn a lot of money —he also wants to... work a lot less!

That is why he constantly follows a law whose very name is music to his ears: the law of least effort...

Let's find out how in the next chapter!

CHAPTER 6

THE LAZY MILLIONAIRE FOLLOWS
THE PRINCIPLE OF LEAST EFFORT

There are several definitions for the principle of least effort...

For most people, it means expending the least amount of effort possible, and staying in your comfort zone for as long as possible...

In screenwriting, there is an interesting law that resembles the line of least resistance. It stipulates that a character only acts if he no longer has a choice not to act, which means that he is only snapped out of his inertia if forced to do so…

For the lazy millionaire, the principle of least effort has another meaning: it essentially means doing as little work as possible to produce the greatest possible financial result…

This law is in fact a corollary, or if you prefer, an elaboration of the famous Pareto principle, which was discovered by Italian economist Vilfredo Pareto, in 1897.

In studying the levels of wealth in England in the 19th Century, he noticed a foreseeable imbalance in its distribution. This finding later led to the famous 80/20 rule, which was developed by George Zipf, a Harvard professor, and Joseph Moses Duran, whose theories were passed over in the United States, but spread through post-war Japan, and produced their spectacular revival.

But what exactly did Pareto discover?

He discovered that 80% of England's wealth in the 19th Century was held by 20% of British subjects, and this is still true in modern society.

Pareto's successors found practical applications for this discovery…

And it's here that any lazy millionaire, whether he is accomplished or just starting out, should pay close attention and take notes...

We all have a tendency, and it's quite frequently a mistake, to think that there is a direct correlation between effort and results.

For example, we assume that 50% of the hours that we work enable us to accomplish 50% of our tasks, and 50% of our efforts generate 50% of our revenues...

So, if we start a business, we expect 50% of our products to be responsible for 50% of our sales; 50% of our employees to be responsible for 50% of our revenues; and 50% of our sales people to be responsible for 50% of our sales and so on...

But in the real world, as Pareto and his successors discovered, there is a foreseeable imbalance between cause and effect.

Overall, experience shows that, on average...

- 20% of our clients are responsible for 80% of our sales,
- 20% of our salespeople are responsible for 80% of our sales,
- 20% of our efforts are responsible for 80% of our success...
- and therefore, despite all of our democratic zeal, good sense advises against distributing our time, energy, and money equitably among our clients, salespeople, and tasks...

The Lazy Millionaire focuses 80% of his efforts and time on clients and activities that are profitable, and sets 20% aside just in case, because you never know...

A small customer can suddenly grow big, or can be bought back by a larger corporation, therefore becoming overnight a large customer...

And when you are starting out, you don't know which customer will eventually become big...

An example of the Pareto's principle?

Book publishing.

Having worked in the industry for half of my life, I know that the 80/20 rule applies nearly perfectly.

For every ten books he publishes, a publisher will see the following results: 3 books will be published at a loss, 3 will break even, 2 will generate a modest profit, and only 2 will be really successful. These two books (especially if they both are real bestsellers) will allow the publisher to end his year with a profit despite the poor performance of 6 out of 10 books, and in fact, closer to 8 out of 10 books.

Publishing is an industry that follows the 80/20 rule to a T, just like the film and music industries, which is why the best-sellers (representing 10% of books published) are found at the entrance at most bookstores, and why 90% of the customers who venture through the doors come to purchase the best-sellers over any other book, because in reality, best-sellers are all they buy.

Major retail chains also follow the law of least effort…
Almost as if by chance, most of them place their cosmetic products at the entrance.

Why?

On the one hand, because more women shop than men, and on the other hand, because these are the products with the highest profit margins.

The benefit is twofold, and illustrates another example of the 80/20 rule, because these are the products that, even though they only occupy 20% or 30% of the entire surface area of the store, are responsible for the largest profits…

You might well ask: "How can you know in advance what books (or in other fields, what products or services) will enjoy exceptional success and generate 80% of your income?"

Well, nobody has a crystal ball, especially in publishing.

I remember the first time I planted rose bushes.
In my zealousness, I bought too many roses for my flower beds, and I had five or six left over. Throwing away roses is a crime against… beauty. Only a barbarian would discard a rose bush!

So with my five or six plants in hand, I noticed that my garden which I wasn't too familiar with yet, had a small piece of land that I thought would not be suited to roses because the soil was poor and sandy.

I planted the roses anyway, telling myself that they would probably only last one season, and that I would have to get rid of them the following summer… But by some strange phenomenon (strange to me because I was only a budding horticulturist), of all my rose bushes, those were the ones that blossomed most spectacularly, year after year.

With my beginner's lack of experience, I didn't realize that the roses I planted first were poorly planted, because I had planted them all along the immense cedar hedges that surrounded my property.

Like many other flowers, rose bushes do not compete well, which means that they tend to suffer, especially if they are up against a hedge that is six metres high and that casts shadows and weakens the soil with its many roots...

In fact, they love the sun, and they also like soil that has a high sand content!

Like the soil in which I planted my last rose bushes, which I thought would wilt!

So when you start a business, do not throw away any rose bushes.

Give a fair chance to all of them.

It's hard to predict which one will produce the nicest roses.

But learn from your experience and try to cultivate what works best for you and bring the nicest and most abundant roses. After all, as every lazy millionaire, you want to smell the roses, yes or no?

Here is how you can use the 80/20 rule in your life and in business in the smartest possible manner...

First, try to determine which of your activities, products, or services generate 80% of your returns...

This exercise is not only useful, but is also necessary if you want to become a lazy millionaire, especially if you have never done it before...

You might be in for a big surprise and you will probably see that, in general, the 80/20 rule will be respected...

Of course, it is important to note that the distribution does not have to be exactly 80/20 in order for the exercise to be useful

You might be at 70/30, or 65/35, or 90/10, or even 99/1!

Once you have a clear picture of the situation, and of the ratio between your efforts and your results, you can take the following actions:

1. if you have established which 20% of your clients constitute 80% of your business, obviously you must try to keep them happy, increase your business with them, and no matter what, be sure that you do not make the mistake of distributing your time evenly between them, i.e. 20% and the other 80% of your clients...

2. try to find new clients (and new employees and salespeople) who correspond to the criteria for your best clients (the 20%), and who will enable you to grow by following the law of least effort...

You should also use the principle of least effort to solve your problems. Take a close look at your problems. You will probably realise that the Pareto law applies here too.

Here is how to use it the lazy millionaire's way:

1. Identify the 15% or 20% or 25% of your clients, employees, salespeople, or suppliers (or tenants if you are in the real estate business) who account for 80% of your problems: bad payers, trouble makers, those who are harmful to the work climate, are unreliable, are late in their work or in their shipments, etc.

2. Then try:
• as quickly as possible (time is money)
• with the minimum amount of effort possible
• by spending the least amount of money possible
• in as permanent a manner as possible …
to improve your clients, employees, salespeople, and suppliers…

Try to bring them up to par with your best, or at least your good clients, salespeople, employees, suppliers...

3. If you fail in Point 2, replace these people as soon as possible!

This may appear cold and harsh, but aren't they the ones who have been harsh with you by treating you so badly in the first place?

All you are doing in the end is exchanging bills for coins!

And you will often be able to avoid serious financial losses or... ulcers!

The lazy millionaire thinks that making money or doing business shouldn't be hard and detrimental to his health. So he acts accordingly by surrounding himself with employees, colleagues, and clients that bring him what he wants in his life.

This being said, do not become a slave of the law of least effort. Life is not only about making money.

A real lazy millionaire knows how to stay human, polite, and nice to everyone he meets, regardless of whether they are able to help him in his efforts as a lazy millionaire or not!

He also knows the truth of the adage: "You never know who you might end up doing business with."

For example, the manager of a publishing house where I regularly do business was just a receptionist when I first met her!

I don't need to tell you that I don't regret having always been polite to her. Of course, it didn't hurt that she was extremely beautiful!

But joking aside, I believe that it is important to always go through life with the attitude that every person we meet is important, and is entitled to receive our full consideration and respect...

But at the same time (there's always a "but", isn't there?), it is important to understand that we can't spend the same amount of time with everyone, or we'd never get through our day...

Every lazy millionaire knows that he must constantly make choices, and make the best possible choices.

Using the Pareto's Law all the time, the lazy millionaire also uses another Law very often.

✂CHAPTER 7

THE LAZY MILLIONAIRE PLAYS ACCORDING TO PARKINSON'S LAW

Parkinson's first law says:

"Work expands so as to fill the time available for its completion."

Humorously explained in the book *The Peter Principle* by C. Northcote Parkinson, the law basically means that:

"To accomplish a task we always use all the time allowed to do it."

For example:

1. Your boss asks you to prepare a report by the end of the month, but it is highly probable that, even if you have three months to complete it, you won't take it seriously until just a few days before the deadline. And you'll probably be adding the finishing touches the night before the deadline.

2. You are a student, and you put in 80% of your study the night before an exam, and 80% of your essay writing time two days before the deadline, if it is not the night before.

3. You are a taxpayer (meaning one who actually pays his taxes!), and even though you have all the papers on hand in February, it is highly probable that you will wait until the last week of April, or even until April 30, before completing and mailing your income tax return, and you will often line up at the post office, which has stayed open until midnight to accommodate the latecomers...

You've had an experience like this, haven't you?

If you really think about it, it's a variation on the application of the Pareto principle, because only 20%, or maybe even less, perhaps 10% or 5% of the time that is allocated is necessary to accomplish 80% or 90% of the task…

Pondering this psychological law, I told myself that I could actually benefit from it!

I told myself that right when I began to earn a living as a "ghost-writer", having left my day job in publishing at the age of 31...

I was paid by the page, so I worked quickly, and the more money I earned, the more time I would be able to "buy" to write my own books!

So I asked myself, as a budding lazy millionaire: "If it's true that, according to Parkinson's Law, we always use all the full amount of the allocated time to do a job, what would happen if I had less time?"

For example, if instead of giving myself 6 months to write a 200-page book (which was what I did before I moved on to become a professional writer), I gave myself only 4...

How would I feel?

Not too stressed, to be honest. (Perhaps now is a good time to admit that I don't stress easily...)

And if, instead of 6 months or 4 months, I only had 3 months to churn out my copy, how would that be?

Once again, how would I feel?

Not much more stressed, in fact...

I pushed this logic a little further, and asked myself what would happen —within my head and my keyboard! - if I were to reduce the time-frame even more...

The first contract I received as a ghost-writer (from an European publisher) was to write a book about... time management!

This was quite a stroke of luck for someone who was always looking for ways to work quickly and effectively!

Before getting started, I had to read a whole crate of books that the publisher had sent me on the topic.

Before reading them, I thought about the best way to do this, and developed a method that I have used ever since. I spent 3 hours quickly scanning the 20 books, in order to determine the order in which to read them.

I made an interesting discovery. In general, there aren't very many good books on any given topic. In fact, only 20% of writers are truly original, and relate approximately 80% of what there is to say about the given topic.

I also noticed that, with the exception of novels, of course, 20% of the text of a book contains 80% of the author's thoughts. And this 20% is conveniently found, for the most part, in the first few paragraphs of each chapter, or even more conveniently, in the form of a summary at the end. The rest of the text constitutes examples, counter-examples, and studies or statistics to support the original thesis!

So I read the best book first, very attentively from cover to cover, and then read the second and third "best" books, faster and faster as their quality was going down and my expertise in the field was growing of course. I was literally flying through the last ones, that generally contained either nothing new or nothing true.

In fact, it could be said about them what one of Freud's now-forgotten detractors said one day after one of his brilliant conferences:
"Some of what you just said is new, and some of it is true. But the things that are true are not new, and the things that are new are not true."

As a result, I read the 20 books in 2 weeks, and without even knowing it, had applied the principles of the lazy millionaire, which proves, if need be, that in order to write fast in this trade, you also need to read fast!

I completed the 200-page book in a month and a half.

I sent the manuscript to the publisher, who was so happy that he sent me a cheque for $20,000!

I had just bought several months of freedom to work on my own book!

I realise that you probably aren't a writer, and you don't have to read a book every day, but it is quite probable that, in your job, you are inundated with reports and with lengthy and detailed studies —in fact with all kinds of documentation… If this is the case, I have a feeling that the lazy millionaire's methods will really come in handy!

When I'm running short on time, I sometimes ask myself the following question when faced with reading a book in order to improve the chapter of one of my books or a conference:

"If you had only one hour to spend in the company of this author and his 200-page book, what would you do?"

The answer: "I would read it in an hour!"

And that's what I do!

And I remember, or at least I absorb, at least 80% of the information in the book.

As for the remaining 20%, I don't think it's worth spending the two or three hours it would take to extract it...

It's the opposite of perfectionism, I know, but remember what Churchill said about this approach, which is often only a disguise for procrastination: "Perfectionism is spelled P A R A L Y S I S!"

Do an experiment with a 30-page report.

Tell yourself:

"If I only had 15 minutes to read this before a meeting, what would I do?"

"I'd read it in 15 minutes!"

And you'll be surprised how much you remember especially if you use speed-reading, a must for a lazy millionaire…

There are many applications of Parkinson's Law, and several of them are often under-estimated.

For example, ask yourself: "If I had to meet with 10 new clients every week, or every day, or every hour, what would I do?"

Take this logic one step further…

Ask yourself: "If I HAD to meet with 300 new clients every day, what would I do?"

Maybe you should take a job as a speaker, and start giving conferences!

Go a little further. Ask yourself:

"If I HAD to reach 500,000 potential clients in one shot what would I do?"

You would try to arrange a television appearance.

Or use an Internet list.

Or put an ad in a major newspaper.

Ask yourself:

"If I only HAD 2 days to prepare my report, instead of the months my boss gave me, what would I do?"

Wouldn't I quickly scan the statistics I needed to report?

Or ask my assistant or my secretary, who is great with numbers, to prepare me a two-page summary, or even a single page?

Or, if I am called upon to enter a new field, or to address the problems of a department for which I have just been made responsible, couldn't I draw inspiration from the example set by J. F. Kennedy?

This outstanding man, who read approximately 1,500 words per minute (the average is 300…), had got into the habit, especially when he wasn't familiar with a topic, of asking the expert he was speaking with:

What are the 10 things I should know about it?

Simple, but brilliant, right?

THE 10 THINGS YOU NEED TO KNOW ABOUT SOMETHING…

Or, if 10 is too many, then 5…

Sometimes, you can simply ask:

"WHAT IS THE MOST IMPORTANT THING I NEED TO KNOW ABOUT THIS TOPIC?"

Or ask experts or successful colleagues these questions or variations of them:

"WHAT IS THE BIGGEST PROBLEM THAT I WILL ENCOUNTER IN THIS FIELD, IN THIS DEPARTMENT, WITH THE STAFF?

Knowing Parkinson's Law, and more importantly, how to use it wisely, can be very liberating.

Why?

Because if you do what everyone else does, and take all the time that is allocated to accomplish a task, I don't think you'll be making the best possible use of your time.

Let me explain why.

Let's say you have one month to complete a task, let's say a report… Chances are not much will be done the first two or three weeks. Probably only 20% of the task will be completed, if not less.

You won't work very hard, but on the other hand your mind will not be free…

Your stress level will gradually increase, reaching its peak in the final days, and before you know it, it's the evening before the big day.

If, instead of allowing this build-up, you tell yourself —regardless of the real deadline —"I only have one week to complete this report…" you will create stress, but it will be good stress, because you always keep in mind the fact that you really have more time.

And, because you complete it during the first week, the remaining three weeks will be your own!

You will sleep better, digest better, live to be older, and be in a better mood.

Because deep down, by redefining the deadline, you will have redefined YOURSELF without even knowing it!

In reality, the deadline given to you by your boss, or by a client, or by a teacher, has become a deadline that YOU set.

YOU are responsible, and you don't have to wait for others to get started.

And I promise you, having experienced this many times over, that it can make an enormous difference in your life!

Here's a little tip, by the way: whatever you do, don't hand the completed report in too far ahead of time!

There are two reasons for this, which you may have guessed or figured out for yourself in the past. The first is that your boss (if you have a boss!) will tend to bombard you immediately with another task, in order to ensure that you aren't twiddling your thumbs at his expense...

The second is that, if he isn't a lazy millionaire, your boss or your client or your partner may think that your report is not as good quality as it would be if you had taken all the time allocated to you, like most people do; even if, in reality, these people use only the final week or even days, and in short, do not work any longer than you.

But only lazy millionaires and aspiring lazy millionaires will understand this!

Obviously, everyone understands that there is a material limit, if you can call it that, when you apply Parkinson's Law.

It would be difficult (I'm not saying impossible) to write 200 (good) pages in 3 days or less, as was commonly done by the great French writer Alexandre Dumas (*The Count of Monte Cristo*, *The Four Musketeers*, etc) thanks to his team of ghostwriters...

You can't sacrifice quality. And you won't have to if you're a lazy millionaire.

Also, you have to keep in mind the fact that you are not applying Parkinson's Law to the point of making yourself sick, but... to gain your freedom!

If you are (or want to become) a lazy millionaire, you know that peace of mind is what you are always looking for first.

So only allow the amount of (good) stress that is necessary to give your mind wings!

There is another way to do more in less time.

Let's see what it is in the next chapter.

CHAPTER 8

THE LAZY MILLIONAIRE LOVES WORK...
THAT OF OTHERS!

Success, as they say, is never accomplished alone.

Neither is fortune.

In fact, very few people became millionaires on their own.

Even in the relatively solitary trades, you need help.

An artist has a manager.

An author has an agent.

Andrew Carnegie, who was one of the wealthiest men in the world in his time, had the following words written on his tombstone: "Here lies a man who was intelligent enough as to hire people more intelligent then himself."

He delegated.

Intelligently.

Which means that he delegated to intelligent people.

More intelligent than himself?

Well...

He certainly didn't hire imbeciles or "yes men"...

He had the intelligence to allow the competition to employ them!

In any case, he was a lazy millionaire to the very core!

Yes, he delegated, with the confidence of a man who wants and knows how to surround himself with strong and competent people.

In his book *Ogilvy On Advertising*, already mentioned, David Ogilvy relates this story:

"When someone is made the head of an office in the Ogilvy & Mather chain, I send him a Matrioshka doll from Gorky. If he has the curiosity to open it, and keep opening it until he comes to the inside of the smallest doll, he finds this message: If each of us hires people who are smaller than

51

we are, we shall become a company of dwarfs. But if each of us hires people who are bigger than we are, we shall become a company of giants."

This concept is at the core of the Lazy Millionaire's hiring philosophy, because he wants a company of giants, and not a company of dwarfs. The Lazy Millionaire wants to surround himself with people who are competent, autonomous, and creative.

Why?

Because, being lazy by definition and by wisdom, he knows that if he employs dwarfs, weak under-performers, and bumblers, or in other words, incompetents, he will be forced to work harder, when he actually made the decision to hire others so that he could work less and earn more money!

He doesn't want to have to constantly check up on the people he employs.

That is not true delegation: it's dissimulated enterprise and obvious self-adulteration. And what you do is this: You say to yourself, more or less consciously: "Those who are around me and who I appointed are less competent than I am, and the proof lies in the fact that I always have to check up on them!"

In one sense, delegating is a sort of spiritual experience: you must trust the other person, and let go, which may be difficult, if not impossible, especially if you are a "control freak"…

In this case, you aren't a lazy millionaire, and you will have trouble getting rich without losing your health and your nerves, and probably your family, too…

All lazy millionaires delegate.

They try to concentrate as much as possible —in fact, exclusively, if possible —on tasks that are at their level...

However, I would like to add the following: when you start out (as an entrepreneur, I mean), you would be well advised to do a lot on your own, and therefore, not to hire too many people too fast. John Paul Getty earned his first million when he was 23, without an office or secretary. He did everything… (including his first million!) out of his car!

Draw inspiration from his frugality and his remarkable sense of economy, and then, as soon as you can… delegate!

But don't delegate just any way: delegate like a lazy millionaire.

The Lazy Millionaire knows that 80% of the key to successful delegation is… choosing the right person.

Therefore, he will not hesitate to dedicate a great deal of time to this task.

He also will not hesitate to spend a lot of time clearly explaining his objectives.

And congratulating the person if the task is accomplished correctly.

Because delegating properly is one thing, but keeping his team's morale up is another: the Lazy Millionaire never forgets this.

In order to delegate effectively, and also to constantly motivate the people around you (employees, associates, colleagues, clients) to increase your popularity and influence, there is a simple tool that 80% of people virtually never use.

Let's look at it together in the next chapter.

You will see that it is truly extraordinary, and its applications are unlimited...

CHAPTER 9

THE LAZY MILLIONAIRE IS POSITIVE

In their wonderful little book called *How Full Is Your Bucket,* Tom Rath and Donald O. Clifton use a simple metaphor to describe human relations.

I will summarize it, because in perfect accordance with the philosophy of the lazy millionaire, it is extraordinarily "economical" in its application, and generates amazing results.

As the authors explain, we all have an **invisible bucket.**

With each one of our interactions —and we generally have hundreds of interactions every day with our boss, our employees, our colleagues, our parents, and our spouses —depending on what people say or do, we feel that our bucket is either more full or less full....

And because we also have an **invisible dipper,** we fill or empty the invisible buckets of others each time we interact with them...

When our bucket is full, or better yet overflowing, we naturally feel good...

And the opposite is true, of course: when it is empty, we feel bad...

Better still, when we fill another person's bucket, we are filling ours at the same time, but when we empty another person's bucket —a trend that is all too common and completely subconscious —we also empty our own bucket…

Haven't you experienced this on several occasions in your own life?

When you say something bad about someone, or criticize them a little meanly, or deliberately refuse to recognize their merit, or when you simply don't listen to them or ignore them, you almost automatically feel smaller, depressed, as if it was you who had been insulted, even subtly, or seemingly insignificantly.

How can we fill another person's invisible bucket?

• By paying a compliment or giving an unexpected gift...
• By offering congratulations for a new appointment or promotion...
• By lending an ear to a friend who is discouraged...
• By spontaneously doing a favour...
• By putting a failure or problem into perspective...
• By surprising someone by doing a good deed...
• By regularly telling someone how much you appreciate his services, partnership, company, or advice...

There are few people who realize to what extent each minor interaction we have each day is influential, because in reality, every moment matters in professional or conjugal life.

American marriage expert John M. Gottman, who wrote the wonderful book *The Seven Principles* for Making Marriage Work, strives to predict the future of a couple, to determine its "sustainability coefficient", simply by observing the way its members interact for just a few minutes.

His observations of several thousand couples over more than 20 years led to this amazing conclusion, which is nonetheless logical when you consider that the magical ratio for interaction in a couple is 5:1.

This means that, if a couple has five positive interactions for each negative interaction, its chances of survival (and therefore conjugal happiness!) are excellent.

The farther the couple strays from this magic ratio, the more its chances for long-term survival and happiness decrease.

When we think that some couples cannot open their mouths without criticizing each other, making negative comments, or mocking their spouse, it's hardly surprising that there are so many divorces and unhappy relationships...

As for me, when I learned about this magic ratio, I realized that I wasn't as positive as I had thought with respect to my contributors, the members of my family, my friends, and my wife, and as a self-respecting lazy millionaire, I quickly made some corrections, which had truly miraculous effects.

Think of your own life…

What is your ratio?

5/1?

7/1?

Or more likely, 3/1?

Or even 1/1, which in reality isn't so bad…

Most people probably have a negative ratio!

Like 3/5 or even 1/5, or worse: 0/5 or 0/10 or 0/20…

Why?

Because —and this is without a doubt the greatest tragedy in the world —8 in 10 people are negative 80% of the time…

Once again, it's Pareto's unavoidable principle!

In fact, when people are not completely negative, they suffer from restricted negativity (like Einstein's restricted relativity!), or maybe they are indifferent, and don't really care about others.

This is why the Lazy Millionaire is an original: he is an edifier…

For him, it's a sport, a mental habit, a system, and it becomes second nature.

He recognizes the work of the people around him, whether they work with him or for him… He compliments them (intelligently and individually!), encourages them, supports them, listens to them, and makes them laugh, often at his own expense, which is even better…

In other words, more often than expected, he fills their invisible buckets...

His success with people, his popularity, his charisma, and his influence are AUTOMATICALLY increased.

Why?

Because survey after survey has demonstrated the same thing: 2 of every 3 employees do not feel appreciated for their work…

It's hardly surprising that this is the number one reason why people quit their jobs…

And we know that departures, which are often hasty and for the purposes of going to work for a competitor, cause concerns, and losses...

Not to mention absenteeism and lack of motivation, which cost American companies more than $300 billion every year!

This is because only people who have never been a good boss believe that people work only for their salary.

Obviously, most of them wouldn't even go to work if they weren't paid (which is quite sad!), but it takes more than a paycheque (especially if it's a small one!) to make people happy and to retain them, because they will feel that they have a chance of being better appreciated somewhere else (even if they are fooling themselves!), and will submit their resignation.

The same applies for a couple: sooner or later, the man or the woman will submit their "resignation" if they do not feel appreciated by their spouse at their full value.

If you want to become an accomplished lazy millionaire, ask yourself immediately what your normal interaction is with others.

Be honest, and be lucid: your success, both financial and personal, depends on it!

Do you fill the buckets of others more often than expected?

Or conversely, are you emptying them without even noticing?

It's important for you to know this, and to make the necessary changes.

Because over the long term, nobody wants to interact with someone who is constantly emptying their bucket...

Unless they are masochistic, or unaware of their value and prepared to accept anything, even the worst hurt feelings!

But that's another story!

By constantly being positive, you will become a magnet to others...

Not only because it's original, because it's like a fresh breeze in the desert of existence and the labour market, but quite simply because it's what everyone is seeking, without even knowing it!

That said, it doesn't mean that you have to be positive ALL THE TIME!

There are moments when we MUST say things that are unpleasant; things that don't make people happy.

But when the intention is good, and when the criticism is constructive, it's acceptable.

Especially if there were previous interactions during which you filled the other's bucket, and there will be others...

Being positive does not mean that you always have to say yes...

For example, in publishing, a publisher may say no to 9 out of 10 manuscripts —perhaps more.

Is that because he is negative? NO.

He might be the most positive publisher in the world, but he knows that good manuscripts are few and far between.

The great movie director Steven Spielberg refused the first three screenplays he was presented for the final Indiana Jones sequel, even though he knew that time was of the essence, and that he would have to find one soon if he didn't want Harrison Ford to play the role from a wheelchair!

Was it because he was negative? NO.

In fact, judging by the extraordinary number of projects that he has developed and his countless successes, he is probably one of the most positive men in his profession.

Murphy's law says: "Anything that can go wrong will go wrong."

In reality, that is what most people think, even if they swear otherwise.

Because they are fundamentally negative.

Without even knowing it.

That's the normal colour of the water in their aquarium, and they can't imagine that it could be otherwise.

The Lazy Millionaire says: "If something can go well, even if there is a chance that it will go wrong, it WILL go well!"

Not only is the Lazy Millionaire fundamentally positive, and not only does he seek a way to triumph, to find an advantage or a benefit in any situation, but he also strives to constantly improve himself.

To constantly and patiently take small steps toward his objective…

He is animated by the kaizen philosophy, which is the Japanese concept for the constant spirit of self-improvement.

If he had known Seneca the Elder, he would say, like him: "It takes the whole of life to learn how to live…"

The lazy millionaire constantly works on himself in order to learn how to live better, and to use the various tools at his disposal more effectively and more subtly: the principle of least effort, which is his favourite; Parkinson's Law, which is useful when it is not abused; delegation, when it is enlightened, etc.

The Lazy Millionaire is POSITIVE.

❧ CHAPTER 10

THE LAZY MILLIONAIRE TACKLES
THE MOST PROFITABLE TASKS FIRST

You probably already know the story of the old Harvard professor who was a time management expert.

But I'm going to tell you again, to illustrate an application that you may not have thought of.

When he started his course, the professor kept a large jar on his desk, which he used as a portable aquarium.

From beneath his desk, he took a box filled with stones as big as his fist, and asked his students:

"How many stones do you think can fit into this jar?"

Everyone made a guess, and then the professor filled the jar, and asked the students:

"Is the jar full?"

Because the professor had trouble fitting the final stone into the jar, everyone agreed that it was full.

The professor smiled and pulled a container of gravel from under his desk, which he began to pour into the spaces between the stones.

Again he asked: "Is the jar full?"

Because they were Harvard students, and they were upset at having been outsmarted the first time, they answered no. With good reason, too, because the professor then proceeded to pour nearly half a pitcher of water into the jar.

At last he asked: "In your opinion, what was I trying to demonstrate with this experiment?"

"That even if we think our schedule is full, it's always possible to add something else, especially AFTER taking your course!" one student ventured.

Amused, the professor smiled again, but gently negated the student's musing.

"No, what I wanted to demonstrate to you was that, if I hadn't put the large stones in first, I would not have been able to put them in at the end, because there would not have been enough room."

Of course, the large stones represent the important things in life...

For the Lazy Millionaire, the important things (in his work, of course) are the things that are most profitable...

Again, this is not because he has an obsession with money. But it is because he is aware of his own personal value, and the value of his time...

He knows that money-making activities, and only money-making activities, will free himself and give him more time... to think about other money-making activities!

And to be able to relax, travel, play golf, learn piano, see friends or simply... do nothing!

He knows that if he lets himself get overwhelmed by "the gravel and water", he won't have enough time for the "large stones", and he will only be able to handle the "small potatoes"?

You see, that's the "virtuous circle" of the Lazy Millionaire!

What about you?

Do you think like that student?

The student who uses time management only to have an even fuller, and therefore more stressful schedule?

Do you fill your jar with gravel and water until there was no room left for the stones?

It wouldn't be surprising if you did, because that's what most people do, and that's why they spend their lives chained to their jobs, and never manage to become lazy millionaires!

They don't realize that, in their jar of life, the water represents the everyday activities, the daily obligations and habits that they think they have to take care of, because ... that is what they have always done!

They don't realize that the gravel represents the emergencies —emergencies that they feel are important simply because they are emergencies, and that devour their time and cause them to lose sight of the things that are really important.

Later on, they are surprised to discover that, if they continue to do what they have always done, they will continue to have the same results as in the past!

For the Lazy Millionaire, the real emergency involves immediately and constantly finding and working on profitable activities...

The Lazy Millionaire does everything in his power to avoid making the mistake that half of American executives make.

Which you might also be making, without even realizing it...

According to a study conducted by Dr. de Woot, a leading U.S. expert in time management, 50% of executives (several of whom had never received training in time management) spend 50% of their time on tasks that their secretary can do!

That's hardly profitable for the company that is paying them!

And it's hardly fair to the secretaries either!

It's not surprising that most executives are overwhelmed!

The important thing for a lazy millionaire is to only agree to do the work that truly reflects his skill level...

as well as clarity, discipline, and maybe a little pride, or at least an idea of your true value, which we must never allow others to diminish. This includes friends, family, and colleagues, all of whom are quite adept at this particular sport...

Do you strive to only work at your true skill level 80% or 90% of the time?

Do you do something that another person could do instead of you, and do even better?

Or are you somewhat masochistic, and because you don't believe in yourself, you act like the most unfair of all bosses, forcing yourself to do the work somebody else could do faster or at a cheaper rate?

It's important to ask yourself these questions.

Really.

If you don't, then you aren't managing your time like a lazy millionaire.

Because you should keep in mind that you don't live forever: you must make the best possible use of every day, every hour.

There will be obstacles, of course.

And in fact, the main one is… YOU!

Because it is quite probable that, at least at the beginning, until you are well acquainted with the principles of the lazy millionaire, you may not feel comfortable working exclusively at your skill level...

You may feel like an acrobat working without a safety net...

Yes, without a net, the old comfortable net, made of all the small tasks that are supposedly so "important" —and not very profitable in fact. The old net made of all the little interruptions that you had been living with for years, which take up your time and keep you from working on the real tasks!

Rockefeller often told his employees:

"Instead of working, loosen your tie, put your feet up on your desk, and ask yourself what you could do to earn more money for your company!"

Write that in you agenda.

Yes, regularly take the time to reflect, to fine-tune your methods, to come up with ideas… that are more profitable!

One per week.

Or at least once per month.

One afternoon, or one morning.

I do it. I call it —the profitable afternoon! T.P.A!

Write it in your agenda exactly like that: T.P.A.

It will become a habit, this time a good one! And you'll look forward to it (especially if the rest of the week has been frustrating), just as you look forward to a weekend that is still days away, or to your coveted two weeks of annual vacation, because you haven't yet learned to always be on vacation, and to liberate yourself from the tyranny of work.

Let me warn you —at the beginning, you'll have a sceptical smile on your face...

But when you succeed in earning $10,000, $50,000, or even $1,000,000 (yes, 7 figures —that's $1 million!!) more per year because of these T.P.A., you will smile again, but this time with confidence and satisfaction!

You will smile, because you will see that THE PROFITABLE AFTER-NOON is not just a series of words that I picked out of the air but a rewarding practice.

When I'm at a conference, I often ask:

"How many people in this room spent an afternoon, or even an hour last month asking themselves, with pencil in hand, how they could make more money?"

In general, not very many people raise their hands —sometimes only one, and then only to ask me to… please repeat the question!

But I am convinced that millionaires, lazy or otherwise, manage their time the same way: by spending a lot of it (and not just one afternoon here or there) doing exactly that. Asking themselves how they could earn more money, more easily, and faster; and how to save on operations, how to improve one of their products (or one of their competitors' products so they can sell it themselves!) and how to provide their clients with better and more effective service...

Yes, millionaires do this most of the time, while those who are not as successful, hardly ever do it.

Essentially, this is the true indicator of wealth.

Not the one defined by the I.R.S (Internal revenue service) in order to track down the tax evaders by trying to determine how many cars you have, how much they cost, how much your house is worth, and whether the salary you are declaring is "logical" considering your lifestyle...

No, in my opinion, the true indicator of a person's (future) wealth (along with his good debts, of course) is the time he spends trying to come up with profitable ideas… That is, until he is wealthy enough to not have to ask financial questions ever again.

Here are a few rules that will help to ensure that your profitable afternoons will be successful:

FIRST RULE

Don't choose a workday, when you are exhausted, for this task.

You need to be at your very best.

You can work when… you are tired!

But when the time comes to think (of profitable ideas) you need to be as fresh as a rose.

In the end, that's how you will be able to smell them!

If you are never as fresh as a rose, it's because you're working too hard…

If you're working too hard, it's because you aren't working effectively...

If you aren't working effectively, you aren't earning enough money...

And if you aren't earning enough money, you won't have any free time...

Do you follow?

So think.

For two hours.

Three hours.

A whole day.

SECOND RULE

Do not allow yourself to be distracted by telephone calls, e-mails, or visitors during this real "work".

THIRD RULE

Do it with a pencil or tape recorder in hand. Or sitting at your computer.

So that you can record your thoughts, analyse and fine-tune them.

FOURTH RULE

You may wish to tackle the task with an advisor or a partner.

Or simply with a friend, who doesn't necessarily have to work in the same field as you.

For instance, I have a friend who is a brilliant businessman and who knows nothing about my field, but who often gives me very useful tips. Of course he is always positive and has a very creative mind that earned him his fortune, because he started with nothing.

FIFTH RULE

Instead of just taking an afternoon or a day, try taking an entire week once in a while!

Spend this week outside your office and outside your home, in a new setting.

Get out of your comfort zone.

Take a trip.

When you are outside of your aquarium, it's easier to see the colour of the water that you have been swimming in for years.

You can bring your spouse with you when you escape, but if you are alone, I am sure you will benefit even more.

Silence is a "magic lamp".

It unravels the most complex issues, and sheds light on the most obscure problems.

If you live as a couple or family, it isn't always easy to find this time, but instead of taking a week, take three or four days. And have the grace to grant the same "mental leave" (like parental leave, only different!) to your partner.

During these profitable afternoons, ask yourself, for example:

"If I had one week - just one week to find a way to increase sales by 20%, 30%, or even 50%, what would I do?"

"If I had one week —just one little week —to earn $5,000 or $10,000 or $100,000 (depending on your level of skill or daring), what would I do?"

It's a fun, and most often a lucrative game, but approach it as if it were really a matter of life or death —or your entire life savings were riding on it!

You don't have a choice.

You HAVE to find a way!

Otherwise, you will… fire yourself!

Not only does the lazy millionaire do the most profitable tasks first, and not only does he often block off profitable afternoons or even weeks in his agenda, but whenever he can (and this is second nature for him!), he strives to make every hour of his time profitable on more than one level…

Yes, on more than one level…

Here is a good example of this way of doing things.

In his book *The Art of the Deal*, billionaire Donald Trump relays the following instructive anecdote:

One day, David Letterman was filming a day in the lives of two American tourists in New York. They were visiting the famous Trump Tower, which houses Donald's offices.

The television host called him to ask if he could pay him a visit.

The billionaire immediately agreed to the meeting.

Five minutes later, Letterman arrived at his office with a cameraman and a couple of tourists, and began to interview him.

Speaking with Trump, Letterman said: "Tell me the truth. It's Friday afternoon, you get a phone call, and you tell us we can come up right away. And you chat with us. Don't you have anything else to do? "

Trump politely replied: "Honestly, you're right. I have absolutely nothing to do!"

It was a joke, of course, because a businessman like Trump, who builds skyscrapers all over the United States, opens (and closes!) casinos, builds golf courses and hotels, receives 1,200 calls per week (obviously, he has a good secretary), and even finds the time to create *The Apprentice* television show, has a pretty tight schedule.

But not so tight that he would pass up the opportunity to spend an hour with David Letterman. Why?

Because this hour was potentially profitable on more than one level:
1. He did the spot because *The Late Show* is watched by millions of Americans every night and a large portion of his success is based on his celebrity status.
2. Trump knew that David Letterman was wealthy enough to eventually buy a condo from him (he said this in his book, not me!). As are the many

rich and famous guests he hosts night after night on his show... Astute, wasn't it?

So when comes the time to manage your time, do these two things:

1. do the most profitable tasks first
2. try to make every hour profitable on more then one level

   In a word, imitate Trump...

   Become ... his apprentice!

CHAPTER 11

THE LAZY MILLIONAIRE ALWAYS STRIVES TO PAY THE LOWEST PRICE

The Lazy Millionaire regularly spends time thinking about ways to earn money quickly and easily.

But that does not mean that he tosses money out the window, and that he doesn't pay attention to the price he pays for the things he buys!

Quite the opposite!

Because he knows that THERE IS NEVER JUST ONE PRICE.

Even at department stores.

In fact, there are ALWAYS different prices.

There is the advertised price, of course, but there are also two or three other prices.

In fact, the only price that the lazy millionaire is prepared to pay is … the lowest price.

Let me give you an example.

Several years ago, I helped my father save $2,800 on a BMW.

I had bought one a few days ago and when I proudly showed it to him, he told me: "That would make a nice Christmas gift for your mother", and he sent me to the dealer to buy it for him.

I went back to the dealer where I wanted to buy my car.

I did not buy it there because the first salesman who greeted me was lacking the most basic manners.

And psychology.

Here's what I mean.

I was wearing my writer's "uniform", which leaves a little to be desired —to say the least!

I have to admit I almost looked like a homeless waif, wearing my wrinkled clothes that really didn't match and three days of stubble on my face!

It would seem that he trusted his first impression.

It should be obvious when someone is serious about making a purchase, no matter what he is wearing!

When I asked the salesman if I could take a look at the BMW 325, he motioned to me with an almost dismissive gesture, saying: "They're over there!"

I went to look at them, alone.

Nobody came to see me for ten minutes.

So I went to another dealer (I'll call him dealer Number 2, who is dealer Number 1's main competitor) and I bought my first BMW.

When it came time to buy a BMW for my mother, I went back to Dealer Number 1 with an idea in mind.

I did not dress any differently than the first time, but I was at the wheel of my brand new BMW.

Which I left in plain sight of the dealer's Number 1 front door.

I went to find the manager, and I said to him: "Do you see that beautiful BMW near the door? Well, last week, when I was shopping around, I came here first, but I was so poorly received that I went to Dealer Number 2 to buy it instead."

His face paled.

"But my father has asked me to buy another BMW for my mother," I continued, "and I wanted to give you a second chance. However, you'll have to give me a good price, because my father is very upset about how you treated me, and the only way I can explain to him why I even came back to see you is if you give me a really good price."

They made me an offer that they didn't even want to put in writing, because… it wasn't their policy.

But they did it anyway.

For me.

Because I explained to them that my father was an accountant, and that he would absolutely need a written document, that he would not take my word for it, and that if they refused, I would be forced to go elsewhere. I did not say where, but they knew! They gave me a detailed estimate, in writing.

I took the estimate to the other dealer instead of my father.

But not right away.

I first explained to him that I had a great price from their competitor, whom they detested.

When I told them the price, they didn't believe me, and said: "That's impossible!" thinking I was bluffing.

I insisted that what I was saying was true, but they still didn't believe me.

So only then did I show them the written estimate.

Sickened at the sight of the written estimate, the dealer immediately called his rival to chastise him, and to accuse him of not playing fair and cutting prices.

This told me that I had a REALLY good price.
So good in fact that Dealer Number 2 was not able to match it.

So I returned to Dealer Number 1, to whom I nobly gave the opportunity to make good.

As a matter of fact, in a mere two hours, I was able to save my father $2,800.

He is wealthy, but he was happy nonetheless.

Very happy.

Because he KNEW that, in order to have the $2,800 in his pocket, he would have had to earn more around $5,000. (We're Canadians, do not forget and pay more then 50% in income taxes)

You may think that such strategies are childish, that people who are truly wealthy don't think or act in such a manner, because they have no time to lose, or would be ashamed to negotiate like rug merchants...

I can't speak for all millionaires, but most of my wealthy friends —and some are worth several hundred million dollars —think and act this way, and always strive to pay the lowest possible price: the lazy millionaire's price.

And you would be surprised to see how thoroughly they negotiate, right to the last dollar.

For them it is a state of mind, a reflex.

Lazy millionaires find no pleasure in paying the full price so they vow never to concede to the first price.

Very often people hesitate to bargain because they do not want to look poor. Lazy millionaires do not mind looking poor. They know they are millionaire or will become millionaire soon. So they let other people pretend they are rich and pay the full price.

71

Lazy millionaires I know often wait until November or December to replace their cars, because they know that this is the time of year when the dealers want to liquidate their inventory in order to make room for new models.

In fact, they will not hesitate to take a model that has served as a demonstrator vehicle (yes, even people who are worth several million dollars!), which the dealer sells at a substantial discount, sometimes 25% of the value of a completely new model.

Intelligent modesty, I find!

The modesty of a lazy millionaire!

Think of all these tips in your life, and in your negotiations.

Never hesitate to ask someone if they can give you a lower price.

The competition is so fierce these days that most merchants give a discount… But you HAVE TO ASK FIRST!

I am never shy to ask for one.

In fact, I S-Y-S-T-E-M-A-T-I-C-A-L-L-Y ask for one.

It has become second nature.

I don't like to pay the full price.

In reality, even though my revenues increase year over year, I JUST FIND EVERYTHING TOO EXPENSIVE!

I must confess that buying a $150,000 house makes me less nervous (and of course less excited)than buying a $500 jacket!

Especially when the house is worth $175,000!

It might sound weird, I know, and it is probably a defect common to a lot of lazy millionaires, but that's the way it is...

Come to think about it, I realize I haven't bought a new jacket for over 5 years! I know, that much is obvious just to look at me, and you were probably about to bring it to my attention —right?

It's easy to pay full price.

Anyone can do it!

I want to pay the lazy millionaire's price.

I'm not saying that I always end up paying the lowest price, but at least I try to.

Some people object, telling me that they don't have time to go shopping and compare, because they are too busy.

I tell them that if they didn't always agree to pay the full price, they wouldn't be forced to work as hard, and they would have more free time… to shop around!

At any rate, I always find the time to do it.

But more importantly, I don't like the thought of throwing my money out the window.

I guess I'm not wealthy enough yet!

So do not hesitate to bargain all the time, in a pleasant manner, as if it was a game. (It is a game in fact!)

And of course, do not forget to do it with the most important items.

It's fine to get a $5 discount on a slightly damaged clothing item, but do not forget to ask for a 1/4 point or even a 1% reduction on a $100,000 mortgage loan, which would allow you to save thousands of dollars. Never believe that the banks have only one rate. Banks are merchants like anyone else, and they don't have one single price.

Always try to keep in mind that the $100 per month that you save on a well-negotiated mortgage loan, for example, represents more than you might believe. In order to get this $100, you must first pay taxes on it. So $100 is $125 or $150 before taxes unless you live in Switzerland or Monaco, or in another country where the "regime" is not as harsh on its taxpayers.

So let's say this meagre monthly saving of $100, on a mortgage, which may seem minute, represents $150 before taxes, so it is $1800 of your annual salary.

If you earn $50,000 per year, this $1,800 represents roughly 3% of your salary. If you look at it that way, it starts to add up, doesn't it?

Add 4 or 5 areas where you could save 3% of your salary in expenses, and you'll achieve a considerable percentage of your salary before taxes. Those who never think of these details (which are really more than just details!) often end up "not making ends meet", as they say, and continually ask how this could possibly happen.

In business, very often the best deal is the DEAL THAT YOU DON'T MAKE!

It's often the same thing when making purchases, especially major ones. You don't always have to do them.

And you don't always have to do them right away.

It will always be possible to spend your money the next day, the next month, the next year.

Money you did NOT spend yet is power, freedom in your hands.

Money you've spent is power, freedom lost.

Of course it takes a modicum of discipline to think and act upon these principles.

But all lazy millionaires I know DO have discipline.

If you do not have discipline, chances are you'll end up like everybody else, instead of investing and saving smartly; you'll spend, spend, spend and probably end up broken and unhappy most of the time.

The other day, an insurance broker tried to sell me $1 million of life insurance, which would cost me just… $250 per month for 10 years! When I told him that I found it expensive, in an effort to make me think about it, and possibly to flatter me at the same time, he said: "What's $250 per month for someone like you who drives a BMW (he visited my home to get me to sign the contract)?"

"It's because I find it expensive that I am able to drive a BMW." I said.

In principle, I'm not against life insurance, and I know that there are many more advantageous plans (for me of course, and not for the company!) than the one the young broker was offering me. Plans where there is something left over at the end, and where your coverage is combined with savings.

But in the end, I did not sign. I am so accustomed to making good "deals", that I knew that I would be signing my death warrant if I signed this contract!

Because I wouldn't be able to keep from dying just to cash in on the $1 million!

The Lazy Millionaire SYSTEMATICALLY shops around, not only in business, where he constantly strives to pay the best price for the best service or the best product, but also in his personal life: for his insurance (home, car, life), and for his telephone, Internet, cable service, etc.

In short, instead of shopping to spend money, as others do, and getting into debt and becoming poorer, set aside your habits temporarily and think like a lazy millionaire: always try to get the best price.

By doing that on a daily basis you will progressively free yourself from the tyranny of work.

Remember, every dollar you save, is a dollar that you can spend later, when you're ready…

It's a dollar that you could invest, and which will grow and multiply…

But even better, if you see it like a lazy millionaire, every dollar saved or invested is one unit of freedom...

A unit of freedom that brings you closer to the 3 or 4 million units you need in order to be free for the rest of your life!

And because you want the rest of your life to start as soon as possible, start to bargain, save and invest as early as possible!

Of course, without becoming maniacal or cheap, for example, by leaving smaller tips at a restaurant...

If you do, you'll no longer come across as a lazy millionaire, but as an old penny pincher, and there are already too many of those around!

CHAPTER 12

THE LAZY MILLIONAIRE TRACKS MINOR, INVISIBLE EXPENSES

Last week, I was surprised when Michel, the owner of the local convenience store, asked a customer $8 for a pack of cigarettes … (It is Canadian prices, of course!)

I have never smoked, because I have never had the means or the health!

"$8 is quite a lot of money!" I said, after the customer left with his cigarettes in hand.

"There's a couple that used to come in here every morning and buy 2 packs because each of them smoked a pack a day," Michel explained.

"They don't come any more?"

"No, they still come, but they stopped smoking a year ago!"

A wise decision, I thought, which enabled them to save $480 per month. (30 times $16 = $480)

$480 per month is a car payment, or a small mortgage…

"Look," announced my friend the convenience store owner. "Here they are now! Speak of the devil…."

They recognized me, and congratulated me on my books, which they said they loved, and added: "We would like to invest in real estate like you suggest, but we don't have any money. Do you have any tips for us?"

"But you stopped smoking a year ago."

"How did you know that?"

"Michel told me."

"Ah."

"So because you were spending approximately $16 per day, you are saving $480 per month, which translates into approximately $5,000. With this $5,000, you could definitely buy a small property using the wise financing techniques that I suggest."

"But we don't have the $5,000!"

I never doubted it, but I just wanted to be sure.

The $5,000 that they saved from not smoking vaporized —in fact, it went up in smoke without them even realizing it!

It's like a set of communicating vessels.

Or a river that is off course, but that runs anyway, only in a different direction!

And it runs in a different direction because it follows another of Parkinson's laws, which says:

"EXPENSES ALWAYS INCREASE IN A MANNER THAT IS DIRECTLY PROPORTIONATE TO REVENUES."

It's scary, but it's true!

Think about your own life as an example...

When you were young, you had a low salary, a small car, and a small apartment.

Now that you are "successful", so to speak, you have a higher salary, a bigger car, and a larger apartment or a house.

But because you have a higher salary, you pay higher taxes.

Because you have a higher salary, credit card companies rush to give you a higher credit limit, which you have maxed out, which has in turn placed the bank at your disposal because of your higher salary!

As a result, you are probably more in debt, and therefore poorer than when you had a lower salary!

Ironic, isn't it?

Yes, like most people (with the exception of lazy millionaires!) the ex-smokers from the convenience store deleted one expense (a pointless and harmful expense) and replaced it with another expense, and so effectively lost track of the $5,000 that their smoking habit cost them previously, but no longer costs them.

$5,000 per year in cigarettes...

It's still money...

Of course, you might say that not everyone smokes and spends $400 on cigarettes every month...

True enough, but if you analyze your other monthly expenses, you may notice that they are filled with "invisible" leaks.

Here is another example:

My friend Michel at the convenience store —him again! —told me that many people spend $20 on lottery tickets every week. That's $80 per month, or close to $1,000 per year, in general, the lottery does not pay the player, which explains the overwhelming profits of all of the world's lotteries!

What's more, he tells me, when he gives them their $2 or $3 change, customers often say: "Give me a lottery ticket instead."

More invisible expenses…

Here are some other examples of these small daily expenses that look like nothing, but that represent large amounts over time …

To stay healthy, it is important to drink a lot of water. For several years, I religiously bought a litre of water for $1.50, which represented a good investment in my health.

(Let me add that we find gas expensive until we pay a lot more for a litre of water —a litre of gas costs approximately one dollar)!

So for me, one litre of water was costing me approximately $45 per month.

My wife did the same thing, so it was actually costing us approximately $100 per month.

Then I realized that, by investing $150 in a home water dispenser, it would only cost me $5 for an 18-litre container!

18 litres, which used to cost me $27, now costs me $5…

It's also better for the environment, because I reuse the same plastic bottle, which I fill myself every morning!
An additional benefit.

Several years ago, at the end of one fiscal year, my accountant revealed to me another one of my invisible expenses by asking me the following question: "Do you know how much you spent in tickets this year?"

"No…"

"$2,100"

I felt sick.

$2,100

That's real money!

At one time in my life, I had the bad habit of believing in my luck (a frequent quirk shared by lazy millionaires!), and telling myself that I would never get tickets: to the extent that I never paid for parking or put coins in parking meters.

The outcome of my blatant disregard was that, at least twice per month, I would receive a ticket. Usually, the fine was only $30, but because I stupidly neglected to pay them on time, they increased, and with the penalties and administrative costs, they rose to the outrageous amount of $85!

So I paid them.

Twice per month, on average, which meant $170.

Multiplied by 12, that's $2,040...

Of course, my company paid the fines (we will see the benefits of running a company in a later chapter), but it was still sickening!

From that day on, I started to feed my parking metres, and to use commercial parking lots.

It cost me money, but a lot less than $2,040 per year...

Take a look at your credit cards.

If you owe $10,000 at a rate of 18%, which is the normal rate charged by most companies, you are spending $1,800.

Furthermore, in order to be able to pay this $1,800, you have to have earned nearly double that amount, or $3,600...

You might want to consider a small consolidation loan with your bank, which might give you a line of credit at 8%. That's a precious $1,000 saved...

I know, I might sound like a fanatic with all these calculations...

These savings may seem petty, but when you add them together, they can have a spectacular effect in the long term...

Take a look at them in your own life, and see how you can save without depriving yourself.

Now let's look at how you can get started, with invisible savings, to put aside a very visible nest egg!

⚘ CHAPTER 13

THE LAZY MILLIONAIRE SAVES
WITHOUT SUFFERING!

Take some goldfish and put them in a pond.

Gold fish that are all approximately the same size.

I did say approximately the same size.

This nuance is paramount, as you will see…

You will see because, if you let a few months go by, a few hot summer months, when you come to look at your goldfish in the fall, you will see that they have undergone a miraculous transformation…

Miraculous because you aren't familiar with the law that I am about to reveal to you…

Yes, you will notice that, even if the goldfish were all approximately the same size at the outset, those that were just a little bit bigger have become MONSTROUSLY HUGE in comparison with their peers.

Who are no longer their peers.

Why does this happen?

Because the tiny difference in size meant that they could swim a little faster than their companions.

It also means that their mouths were a little bigger…

And these two small advantages combined allowed them to consume an astonishingly larger quantity of food than their rivals in the great race of life…

Which is why they grew to be so big!

That is also why you should never turn your nose up at small gains —the small investments and savings that you make daily —because over the months and years, they can help you to become the biggest fish in the pond!

Or in any case, a bigger fish than those who don't use this approach.

Obviously, the earlier in your life you start to practice the virtues of saving (and investment, of course!), the faster you will free yourself from the tyranny of work in order to become a lazy millionaire.

Remind yourself that it is never too late to start.

Why?

Because in most developed countries, longevity increases each year.

So even if you start to save when you're 40 or 50 years old, this is excellent, because there is a chance that you will live to be 80, 90, or even 100 years old!

If you are 20 years old today, you will probably live to be 100, and those who are born in 2006 will probably live to be 125!

However, I must add this proviso: if obesity and sedentary lifestyles continue to prevail in the new generation, it may not live as long as ours!

At first sight, this may be a relief to the government, who will not have to pay old-age pensions for quite so long... But —and there is always a "but", and this is a big fat one, so to speak —obesity causes nearly 1/2 of all diseases (diabetes, heart disease, cancer, rheumatism, stroke, etc.), and therefore, it will cause healthcare costs to explode. This is the equivalent of squaring the circle for governments, who lose either way!

But let's return to our more optimistic scenario, in which people, who are suddenly hit by the good sense to eat less and exercise more, will live longer.

How is longevity such as this possible?

Thanks to the progress in medicine and technology, which will be able to replace your entire body!

Heart, kidneys, eyes, hair, skin, hips: these are already replaceable.
But we'll go even further.

They'll be able to replace your limbs, your sex organs, the most important of which is your brain.

They'll insert a chip into one of your lobes that will provide you with as much memory as the most powerful computer in the world!

Another chip will be inserted to relieve the trembling caused by Parkinson's disease (this has already been invented).

A small manufacturing plant will be surgically attached, producing a constant supply of antibodies to prevent the assault of cancer by destroying precancerous cells...

A Prozac plant will be added to regulate your moods...

Another will fight bad cholesterol, and will clean your blood every day, just like filtration plants purify the water you drink...

A computer that is linked to your doctor's network will be implanted (or worn on your wrist) that will constantly monitor your heart rate, your blood pressure, and the condition of your arteries and organs, and your doctor will know everything about you and the state of your health, without a visit...

In reality, if you were Indiana Jones, once you reach a certain age (advanced) you would be nothing more than the mere memory of Indiana Jones!

Nearly everything that you were born with will have been replaced. Except for your genetic code, which may have been modified at your request... or at the request of your spouse, who wants to pass on a better genetic heritage to her progeny.

(To learn more about this fascinating futuristic scenario, read Eirik Newth's book *A Brief History of the Future*).

But of course...

These changes will cost money.

A lot of money.

Those who do not want to die will have to... pay!

From their own pockets.

In fact, the future has already begun.

It's called two-tiered medicine.

This is a friendly euphemism that hides what it really is, and what it will continue to thrive as: medicine for two budgets!

What will people do if they are not lazy millionaires, or ordinary millionaires, or "middle class", as they are referred to?

I have to ask myself that question.

It's up to you, and not the government, which is already in debt over its head, to take the necessary measures to protect your future.

And to do it at an age where you are energetic, imaginative, and bold enough to generate sufficient revenue to invest and to save.

Some people, instead of making an effort to increase their revenue and to strive for financial independence as quickly as possible, give into the popular trend called voluntary simplicity.

To put it simply, they would rather tighten their belts, reduce their expenses, or "downsize", to use a buzzword, instead of working harder to generate more revenue.

Yesterday, I saw a young, forty-something bachelorette on television who was living, by choice, in a small one-and-a-half, and who bragged about working part-time in order to be able to enjoy life. Good for her! But when she is 60 or 70, and possibly ill, and may have lost her part-time job, and has not put any savings aside, will she still like her situation and brag about it, or will she bitterly regret the folly of her youth? Will she still be able to "enjoy life", or will she be forced to live at the mercy of a government that is increasingly less generous?

In the game of money, there are two approaches: defence and offence.

Defence means saving, living below your means...

In baseball, they say: "Pitching is the name of the game..."

If you don't have good pitching, you don't win.

The same applies in hockey: no team can aspire to be the greatest, which means winning the Stanley Cup, unless it has a great goaltender.

It's great to score 5 goals, but if your goalie lets in 6, you still lose...

The same is true with money: if you earn $300,000, but you spend $400,000, you have a problem!

This is the problem with voluntary simplicity.

The defence is impressive, but the offence is defective.

It's true that it is possible to reduce our needs (especially if they are artificial), and to do without a luxury vehicle, or even any vehicle at all, to sacrifice our second home, to keep our primary residence to a minimum (like the forty-something young lady in my example), to eliminate restaurants, nice clothes, golf, travel, and all forms of fun...

In a word, it is possible to be ultra-defensive.

But choosing voluntary simplicity also means immediately renouncing all plans to take exotic vacations, to buy a Nikon, to see a show on Broadway, to visit Tokyo, Venice, Rio de Janeiro, or Moscow...

Isn't that's a little discouraging?

Your little pad is nice, and you say you have everything, but still...

What concerns me most with this philosophy is the long-term consequences: because you use every dollar to live or "get by", and you are not able to put much, if anything, aside.

Woody Allen said: "Eternity is really long, especially near the end."

Voluntary simplicity enthusiasts would probably say, in their final stretch of life: "Retirement is really long... especially near the end!"

Especially if it lasts 20, or 30, or even 40 years, and old-age pensions gradually disappear like the grin of the Cheshire cat.

The lazy millionaire constantly strives to work on his defence and on his offence, but in a balanced way.

In terms of defence, he is particularly attentive to the stunning virtues of savings...

I was recently chatting with a long-time friend, who has a terrible weight problem.

I told him: "Maurice, you should look at it this way. Life is suffering, as the Buddhists say. But that's good news if you look at it the right way."

'What?"

"Let me explain."

"I'm listening."

"You know that you will suffer one way or another. But you have the choice about how and when."

"What?"

"It's simple. In fact, it's even mathematical… You can choose to suffer immediately, by forcing yourself to go on a diet and to exercise; or you can choose to suffer later, but without being able to choose the exact moment, by continuing to do what you're doing, and inevitably getting sick. What's more, you risk being in a lot more pain. Think about it. It's your choice."

Fast and constant savings, and investment, is the lazy millionaire's hygiene. It's his diet, his daily gymnastics. This is his voluntary suffering in order to ensure that he does not suffer later, and to maintain good financial health.

I know, there are some people who say: "I don't want to save anything. Saving is for the cautious and for old people. I want to live for today, make the most of it, and spend everything I earn. After all, I might get killed crossing the street in three years, so why deprive myself?"

The problem is that they don't die in three years! They survive.

It reminds me of people who smoke.

You tell them (and they've already heard it a thousand times): "You shouldn't smoke, it's bad for your lungs and your heart, and it has been proven that it causes cancer."

They say: "My grandfather smoked, and he died when he was 95!"

"But every year, thousands of people die from smoking well before they turn 90, and even second-hand smoke is dangerous."

"Well, everyone has to die from something!"

I agree with them.

Everyone has to die from something.

But what these people forget is that, during the final ten or fifteen years of their lives, many of them will suffer from emphysema, or will undergo a procedure to remove their larynx because of cancer, and will have a hole in their throat in order to be able to speak at all.

And they might figure out that they were not quite so smart: they forgot that dying from something is one thing, because dying is inevitable, but being sick for ten or fifteen years because they smoked like a chimney is another thing that could have been avoided, and something that is certainly not pleasant.

If they used reasoning similar to how the lazy millionaire disciplines himself, and worked on their defence, and invested, and saved...

But interest rates are so low, you might say, especially if you live in Japan, where the lending rate has not exceeded 1% for several years ...

At the end of 2005, a bank in my neighbourhood offered the following program:

A 7.5% interest rate, which is very attractive these days, if you deposit a fixed amount every two weeks for at least 5 years.

The advertising brochure gave the following examples:

By depositing $50 every two weeks, you will have the following amounts at the end of the following time periods:

5 years: $7,749;

10 years: $18,617;

15 years: $33,860;

20 years: $55,239.

I realize that it takes time, ...

It's not the investment of the century!

It doesn't hold a candle to the $1,000 US that you may have invested in 1965 in Berkshire Hathaway Inc., which is the company that was founded by Warren Buffet, who is the second wealthiest man in the United States. Today, in 2006, that same $1,000 is worth the incredible amount of $5,500,000!

Yes, more than $5 million —you read it right!

Berkshire stock has tripled over the past 10 years alone.

I would advise you to buy some shares, but they are very hard to acquire for the small-time investor, selling for approximately $90,000 US per share!

But let's get back to our little investment.

You can't do much with $55,239, and besides, what will $55,239 be worth in 20 years, in 2025 dollars, when you consider inflation!

Much, much less than today, I know…

You have a good point!

I don't disagree - $55,000 isn't much, it's no Fort Knox!

On the other hand, all of the lazy millionaires I know demonstrated frugality and foresight, living well below their means, and saving in one way or another, at least when they started out, and often for many years. Anyone can spend everything they earn.

In fact, most people spend MORE than they earn.

Which is the real reason why they have financial problems, and not because they don't earn enough.

This is true even for those who earn $100,000 or $300,000 per year!

This is also why we often read stories in the newspapers about artists who, after being rich and famous, are ruined. If these spend-happy artists had controlled their expenses just a little during their glory years, if they had saved even 15% of their unfathomable income, like lazy millionaires do systematically, they wouldn't be in this position, faced with bankruptcy and virtually forced to beg.

Some artists have allowed their managers to handle their affairs. And we know the results of this!

The lazy millionaire, even if he is an artist, and even if he has financial advisors and a manager, takes care of his own affairs, or at the very least, oversees them.

He knows that, even if he isn't the greatest financier or accountant in the world, and even if he occasionally makes mistakes, he will never steal from himself!

By monitoring his expenses, by eliminating pointless expenses, by constantly spending less than he earns, the lazy millionaire gradually frees himself from the tyranny of work, while others are forced to work virtually until their death, which often leads them to die before their time!

But I can still hear you: $55,000 at the end of 20 years, it's not enough…

I agree: so instead of $50, set aside $150 every two weeks. Now look at what you end up with…

5 years: $23,534;

10 years: $57,320;

15 years: $105,825;

20 years: $175,459.

$175,000...

That's better...

It's still not that much, you might say, but it's more than the amount of savings that many people have at retirement, in fact, one in two people in America…

You may also say that you are just barely making ends meet, and sometimes not even that, and because of that, you don't have the $50, not to mention the $150 that this program calls for every two weeks.

In order to offset this objection, which isn't really valid, you could refer to the sausage technique.

What is the sausage technique?

It's a time management method that suggests that, when we are overcome by the overwhelming scope of a task, we divided it into small portions, like a sausage.

It works —you'll see.

For example, if I ask you:

"Could you put aside $300 per month?" You'll probably say: "No, that's too much!"

But if I ask you:

"Could you put aside $10 per day?" You'll probably say: "Yes, I could do that, $10 is nothing!"

Ten dollars per day, how much is that when you stop to think about it?

A glass of house wine at a restaurant costs $7...

With taxes and tip, we will often leave $10 on the counter, especially if the waitress is nice, and of course, pretty.

$10...

This is the $10 that you need every day…

Yes, most people have $10 per day…

At any rate, most have $50 every 2 weeks, which is the $100 per month that they need to subscribe the program I just told you about.

You have it too.

At least if you are an average North-American in terms of revenue and consumer habits...

$100 per month is a meal at a restaurant; a meal that you could skip.

You won't die! And your waistline will probably thank you…

$100 is 6 or 7 bottles of wine per month. If you already drink one per day with your spouse, like my wife and I did for years, you'll be left with 23 or 24 bottles per month —it goes unnoticed: and it will be much better for your liver and your weight!

Just think about all the invisible expenses that we identified in the previous chapter, which you could eliminate if you started to save...

If saving seems boring to you, and seems like an unadventurous way to go, think of it like jogging.

When we see people jogging, we often ask ourselves why they are jogging: they're already so thin! (I don't ask that, because I have been jogging since I was 16, without even missing one week, even when I've been sick!) The clear answer is that they are thin because… they jog!

It's the same when people ask themselves how lazy millionaires can save —it's the reason why they are millionaires!

It's exactly because they saved and invested (often starting very young in their lives!) that they became wealthy, and are even wealthier today!

Like the slightly bigger goldfish, which had only a small advantage over the others at the outset, but which became immeasurably bigger!

You pay bills, accounts, property tax, and a variety of other taxes every week, or at least every month.

But you don't pay yourself, as we say in financial terms.

The lazy millionaire does it all the time.

HE PAYS HIMSELF FIRST.

Imitate him.

Do what all lazy millionaires recommend to their young —and older —disciples: put 15% of your salary before taxes away, by taking it (or having it taken) directly off your paycheque.

That way, you will be guaranteed (like insurance coverage) that you will be able to live below your means, instead of living above your means.

In addition, if a portion of this 15% "forced" savings allows you to subscribe to a tax deductible retirement savings plan, as is the case in our tax system, then so much the better!

What you must remember is that… You won't suffer!

YOU WON'T EVEN NOTICE THAT YOU HAVE LESS MONEY AVAILABLE: you would have spent it elsewhere anyway!

In fact, you will gradually start to feel better.

It's like going on a diet that involves consuming 300 calories less, yes, only 300 calories less per day, which is one piece of cake, one beer, or one bag of chips!

Just look at how much thinner you will be at the end of the year!

You will feel better, because little by little, without even noticing it, you will have:

1. a small cushion (inflatable) in case of hard times: illness, unemployment, divorce, recession;

2. the capital you need to start up a business or make an investment;

3. a pension for your golden years, which will help to make your retirement a little more golden;

4. the $15,000 or $30,000 you need for that trip you've always dreamed of, but wouldn't be able to take otherwise.

So start saving right now. You won't feel a thing, but you will soon become the biggest gold fish in the pond…

✄ CHAPTER 14

THE LAZY MILLIONAIRE LIVES
LIKE A KING ON A BEGGAR'S SALARY

In their fascinating book *The Millionaire Next Door*, the authors draw portraits of "invisible" millionaires, or at least millionaires who are less flamboyant, and they cite the following numbers:

66% of millionaires work for themselves…

Of this number:

75% are entrepreneurs, and…

25% are professionals, such as lawyers, doctors, dentists, etc.

The Lazy Millionaire sees another benefit in having his own company whether it is for him a full time job or not.

This way, he can live like a king on a beggar's salary.

The thing is, being self-employed has tax benefits that are often quite surprising.

a. You can have (at least in many countries) an expense account for lunches, gas, and hockey tickets, for example, and it's even better when your clients are also your friends…

b. You can travel on company expenses for business trips, of course, but you still have the right to take a peek at the Eiffel Tower when you decide to rub shoulders or do some prospecting in Paris! Do you follow?

c. Your business can pay for your cell phone, your regular phone line, and your Internet connection. If you work at home, your company can pay for part of your rent or your mortgage, your insurance, your heating, and your electricity.

You can have a company car that you use for business. I know it's a taxable benefit under certain circumstances, but if you already have a personal car, a car that may even be used and older, and worth almost noth-

91

ing —one that was paid for a long time ago, your second car —, which is your company car, is not a taxable benefit. Do you follow?

How can this be beneficial —even very beneficial?
Because if you don't have a company, your travel, all your meals, your cell phone, and your Internet access —all of this —ALL OF IT —is paid for with AFTER TAXES DOLLARS.

Take the example of paying for your car, which you lease and which costs you $500 per month. You basically have to earn more or less $750 ($1000 in Canada!) before taxes in order to make your monthly payment, which means that $9,000 of your gross salary goes toward paying for your vehicle.

However, if your company pays for the car, the $500 is an expense —a $6,000 per year expense, and these dollars are not taxable since they are deducted from your profits. (Of course your company renting a car may cost you a little bit in taxes, but you will still save...)

Your company also pays for your car insurance.
Let's say $1,000 per year...
You would need to earn roughly $1,500 to pay this...
And I haven't even mentioned repairs...

In fact, all of these tips, which are perfectly legal, can make a HUGE difference in your life.

You can live better by paying yourself a far lower salary.
In fact, you can live like a king on a beggar's salary?!
One day, when I was first starting out, a friend, who was in fact a great lazy millionaire nearing the end of his days, told me:

"When you really start making money, you spend nearly as much time trying to find ways to pay less taxes as you spend making money!"

He was talking about perfectly legal ways.
All governments spend most of their time seeking new ways (disguised or otherwise) to tax us. And when we get the impression (naïve as it is!) that they are giving us a gift (normally during an election campaign), they hasten to take away with one hand what they give out with the other.

So is it not perfectly legitimate for us to seek legal ways to defend ourselves from constant "fiscal attacks", and to pay a little less in taxes?

Here are some other examples of ways to defend ourselves:

Your company can pay you dividends instead of a salary: the income tax rate is lower.

Your company can practice a perfectly legal form of fiscal averaging, by not necessarily paying you a high salary because it posted high profits in a given year. The taxation rate is generally lower for a company, and you can pay yourself later, at a time of YOUR choice, for example, at a time when you may have less revenue from other sources, or when you have losses you can apply against your revenues that year…

Under certain conditions, you can also split your income by paying a salary to your spouse or to your children, which represents another legitimate form of tax relief for you, especially if your spouse is at a lower tax rate than you are.

Some people turn to trusts, holdings, foundations…

But since I am not a tax planner, I won't dwell on these matters any longer, because they vary from one country to another.

I only want you to remember the general principle.

A Lazy Millionaire (like any millionaire!) constantly strives to profit from all the fiscal benefits that the government offers to people who are self-employed.

Because if we think about it for a few moments, it suddenly comes crystal clear:

THE MONEY THAT WE SAVE IN TAXES
IS THE MONEY THAT IS MOST EASILY EARNED

It's also the most fun to earn, because it is the money that costs us the most to give to the government, year after year.

I realize that, deep down, we should rejoice at having to pay $1 million or $2 million or $5 million in taxes, because it means that we must have earned $ 1.5 million or $3 million or $7 million during the year… But I have never seen anyone offer a champagne toast after sending a hefty tax cheque to the government!

Yes, the money we save in taxes is precious to us, as if we are able to subtly pull it from our pockets right before the government snatches it away!

That, I believe, is why this money makes so many lazy millionaires happy.

Because who likes to be duped?

This "fiscal attention" is just another method that the Lazy Millionaire uses to monitor his expenses: because taxes ARE an expense, we should never forget that. In fact, taxes represent one of the most damaging expenses, especially for those who are not equipped for the battle.

If you think about it —but not for too long, because you'll only get depressed! —you work from January until April (even May or June in some countries) just for the government, and I mean just to pay your taxes.

A final note. You may say: this is very well and I wish I had a company to benefit all that but I'm just an employee.

Don't forget that you don't need to work for yourself exclusively to have a company.

You can be an employee AND have a company.

And enjoy the tax benefits.

Think about it...

All lazy millionaires think this way.

This is one of the reasons they can live the life they live even with an income that is often far from being extraordinary.

✀ CHAPTER 15

THE LAZY MILLIONAIRE
TRUSTS HIS INTUITION

One day, my publisher and I met with a promoter who was organising a motivational event featuring a number of speakers, including some as prestigious as Jack Canfield, co-author of the popular *Chicken Soup for the Soul* series, Les Brown, Janet Lapp, and a few others, including yours truly.

I had an idea that could double my fee as a speaker:
the publisher would print and sell to the promoter 10,000 copies of my yet unpublished book, *The Golfer and the Millionaire*, which could serve as a gift book for the event. Since I would make 1$ a book in royalties, well it was easy to figure out the leverage of this idea…

The publisher was thrilled too since it meant 10,000 copies sold right away and a free and sensational launch for the book.

A launching that would make money instead of costing money: again the "differential"… As a matter of fact I think a lazy millionaire always tries to turn something that cost money into something that makes money —and it is possible more often then we think!

So we met for lunch with the promoter, whom I will call Sergio, even though he wasn't Italian.

He had a dark tan, and announced to us that he had just returned from a 3-week vacation in Mexico.

Everyone is entitled to take a vacation, but his announcement irked me, because the event was barely six weeks away, and it seemed like he was being a little reckless by taking off for such a long time before an event that was expected to be attended by 10,000 people.

We chatted for a while, and the publisher handed Sergio the contract.

I offered my Mont Blanc pen, and added as a joke, but also to speed up his decision, yet without really believing that it would be effective: "Do you want to sign with my pen or yours?"

After a moment of hesitation, he replied "I'll use yours…".

And with that, he signed the contract, without even reading it!

Again, I wasn't sure what to think.

My intuition told me that this was not normal behaviour.

Unless it was a contract that he had already signed dozens of times with the same company, any businessman worthy of the title never signs a contract without at the very least having it looked over or seen by his legal advisor.

I followed this reasoning: If a man signs a contract in such a cavalier manner that it seems like the contract has no value to him, then there is a strong chance that he won't honour it.

During lunch, I gently insisted that I be paid up front as a speaker. The promoter agreed to sign a cheque dated the day before the event. Relieved, I slipped it into my pocket.

When we left the lunch, I shared my thoughts with the publisher, and strongly recommended that he not deliver the 10,000 books UNTIL AF-TER he got paid for them.

Surprised, he asked me why I was suspicious of the promoter, whom he had found to be charming and honest beyond his suspicions. He was taken aback to hear such mistrust coming from Marc Fisher, someone who is supposed to be always POSITIVE. I told him exactly what I just told you, about my intuition. We each went our way.

Time passed. The day before the event, still guided by my intuition, I went to Sergio's bank to have the cheque certified. I had a vague eerie feeling that he might not have the funds in his account. But he did! I breathed easier, and told myself that perhaps my mistrust was unfounded, and that I probably should have ignored my intuition. That same day, the publisher called me to gently tease me because he hadn't had any problems getting paid for the 10,000 copies before delivery. Obviously, I had been paranoid. I apologised honourably. Well, everybody can be wrong once in a while…

But the day after the event, the phone rang again. It was the publisher, calling to tell me that we had got off "lucky".

The government the day of the event had seized all of Sergio's accounts because he owed a fortune in unpaid taxes! The crafty tax officials had waited until Sergio had received all of the money from the participants before striking!

As a result, none of the cheques that the speakers received the day of the event could be honoured!

My intuition hadn't warned me that Sergio was in trouble with his taxes, but it had warned me that he was a very unusual businessman…

My intuition had warned me of an imminent danger!

And because I listened to it —and thanks to a bit of good luck —I wasn't affected! I was the only speaker to be paid in full!!

In addition, I had probably prevented my friend the publisher from suffering a heavy loss, because the promoter declared bankruptcy just one week later!

By following my intuition, like any true lazy millionaire, I had avoided a personal loss of $20,000… and helped a friend avoid a loss, too.

So in a way I made $20,000 in what… 5 seconds? 10 seconds? —if we forget the time it took me to go to the bank to have the questionable cheque certified!

How much does it make an hour?

In fact, the work of my intuition generated even more in income because my friend, the publisher, avoided a loss of more then $25,000.

In his brilliant book entitled *Blink*, Malcom Gladwell writes: "We live in a world that assumes that the quality of a decision is directly related to the time and effort that went into it."

The talented young *New Yorker* writer made this insightful reflection after he noted the surprising results of a study that I will explain below.

One day, psychologist Nalini Ambady showed students three ten-second videocassettes of a professor with the sound off, and the opinions of the students were consistent. Ambady then cut the tapes down to five seconds, and the evaluations essentially remained the same. They remained remarkably identical when she showed the students videos that lasted only two seconds. Ambady then compared these "instant" evaluations with evaluations of the same professors that were provided by students who had spent an entire semester in their classes, only to find that the evaluations were all consistent. According to Gladwell, this is representative of the adaptable power of our subconscious mind.

Or in other words, it's the extraordinarily economical power and wisdom of intuition.

Which is behind the lazy millionaire's delights —and fortune.

Why do so few people trust their intuition?

Undoubtedly, it's because we live in a world where the left side of the brain (for righties) is often deemed to be more important: the side that controls rationality and logic...

If it isn't scientific or empirical, it can't be trusted —it's nothing more than an old wives' tale!!

In his fascinating work entitled *The Psychopathology of Everyday Life*, Freud makes very enlightening comments about intuition and about the degradation of its importance with the advent of scientific thought and "progress".

"The Roman who gave up an important undertaking because he sighted an ill-omened flock of birds was superstitious. But if he withdrew from an undertaking because he had stumbled on his threshold, he was absolutely superior to us unbelievers. He was a better psychologist than we are striving to become. For his stumbling demonstrate to him the existence of a doubt, an internal counter-current the force of which could weaken the power of his intention at the moment of its execution. For only by concentrating all psychic forces on the desired aim can one be assured of perfect success."

In other words, when the Lazy Millionaire reads his horoscope —if of course he has the time and inclination to do so! —and he is told, like every other Aries or Leo in the world is told, that he must abstain from making any important decisions on that day because Jupiter is casting a negative influence, he knows that it would be far too superstitious of him to stay home in bed.

However, if by some flukes he takes three wrong turns on the way (even though he knows the area well!) to signing an important contract with a new client, or if he can't find his keys, he might consider this is his intuition, which is (far more) cleverer than he is, trying to tell him something, sending him a sign to NOT go and sign the contract that may appear to be lucrative, but which could be devastating because the client will never pay or will cause so many problems he wished he'd never signed him up.

You may not have a good "feeling" when you meet someone for the first time, even though you have only heard good things about the person...

A little bird tells you that an employee or a patron has not been honest, so much so that he can't look you in the eye when he's speaking to you...

98

I'm sure that you know what I'm talking about...

In any case, the Lazy Millionaire is always on the lookout for these signs: listening to his intuition saves him time and money.

But make sure you take the time to do your homework and check things out, even if it is just a quick check, before you jump in and invest your last dollar in an adventure you feel good about!

However, I would like to add a proviso: if your intuition ALWAYS tells you that ALL of your projects are pointless, and that EVERY person you meet is dishonest or incompetent, you should question it.

You are probably more negative then you think.

So begin right away your education as a lazy millionaire!

Only then will you be able to rely on your intuition.

❧ CHAPTER 16

GIVE YOURSELF A LAZY MILLIONAIRE'S AGENDA

"Great geniuses often produce more by working less," Leonardo da Vinci once said.

These sound like the words of a true lazy millionaire!

And because they were uttered by one of the greatest minds of all times, it's important to listen carefully. Like the advice that he gives in *A Treatise on Painting*: "Every now and then go away, have a little relaxation, for when you come back to your work your judgment will be surer, because by working constantly, you lose the ability to judge effectively...."

So not only should you do what you like to do, but rest often and take frequent vacations!

That's what the greatest achievers do.

Why do you think Tiger Woods doesn't play in all the tournaments, just like the great Jack Nicklaus before him?

Because, like his illustrious predecessor, he knows that it is not possible to have the energy, intensity, and concentration necessary to win week after week —and more importantly, to win the major tournaments, which are milestones in his career.

So he takes care of himself.

He manages his efforts and his rest effectively.

Like a lazy millionaire.

Because the Lazy Millionaire knows that his most valuable assets are his time, and his... ENERGY!

Without energy, and especially without the highest, purest, and most vital form of energy, he will never be able to achieve great things and make money the lazy millionaire way.

Without energy, he will not be able to have clear ideas.

Without energy, he will not be able to come up with a million-dollar idea.

Without energy, he will be like most people, which do not see and seize an opportunity because they are exhausted from work!

Without energy, he will not be able to avoid costly errors in judgement.

Without energy, he will not be able to convince those around him to join him in the direction that he has chosen: that of fortune and success.

So he protects his energy like a real treasure.

In a way, instead of managing his time, the lazy millionaire manages his energy.

Mark Twain once said: "Everybody talks about the weather, but nobody does anything about it!"

Couldn't we make the same comment about work?

Everybody talks (and complains!) about having to work so much, but nobody takes vacation often enough.

The Lazy Millionaire does not complain, because it is part of his life discipline to not exceed his limits and to take care of himself.

Contrary to popular belief, people who worked too much are constantly LACKING IN SELF-DISCIPLINE!

It's for this very reason, because he is disciplined, that the Lazy Millionaire SERIOUSLY plans his vacations in his agenda…

And seriously means often…

In fact, every time you start to feel stressed, negative, moody, depressed… that means that it's time to stop! (If you have felt this way for years, then you have a lot of catching up to do!)

Because your body is telling you something.

Your body is telling you that if you don't take a vacation, it will take one for you!

Without your consent: you will get sick!

If you don't take care of it, it will take care of you!

Which do you prefer?

Lying tanned on a beach with good company nursing a margarita, or lying in your bed alone nursing a high fever?

So do not waste to much time working unless is a game for you.

Instead live like a lazy millionaire.

PART II

THE ART OF ALWAYS BEING ON VACATION

✂ CHAPTER 1

TAKE YOUR TIME, BECAUSE… IT'S YOUR TIME!

They say that "time is money".

If that's true, then I have bad news for most of you: I get the impression that you don't have much money because …

Because ten or twenty times a day, I hear people around me complaining: "I don't have time!"

"I'd like to exercise, read the latest best-seller, or spend more time with my children but… I don't have time!"

"I'd like to travel more, play more golf, take a vacation, but… I don't have time!"

"I'd like to see my cousins or aunts more often than once every thee or five years, but… I don't have time!"

And every time you bury an old uncle or aunt, you promise yourself that you will make an attempt to see your relatives in places other than a funeral home.

But the next time, somewhat amused, and feeling terribly guilty, you remind each other that you made the same promise the last time you saw each other, that these weren't just empty promises: that you will get together under better circumstances!

Nevertheless, if there are no baptisms or weddings in the family, you don't see each other: you have to wait until the next funeral!

We are all in a Grand Prix race, a Grand Prix that is increasingly more expensive...

That's normal —it's a Grand Prix, which can be literally translated as Large Price!

So each day you have to drive faster and faster, right up to the last lap, which sometimes comes sooner than you ever expected!

For all intents and purposes, as they say, you walked into your life at the age of twenty, moved into or prepared to move into your first apartment, because your parents were anxious for you to … get your own life and spread your wings, so that they could spread their wings again and start living again!

You burn the candle at both ends, because you are studying AND working… so that you can pay for your education and cover all of your other expenses. For the first time in your life, you understand why your father yelled at you all through your teenage years to… turn off the lights: the cost of electricity is outrageous!

And you feel that certain sadness when you think of your father, whom you always perceived as a maniac and a penny-pincher.

You drive behind the wheel of a tiny, rusted out Honda that you absolutely love, because it's your first car, and because it just keeps going, and costs very little in gas...

At the age of twenty-five, you finally have your first "real" job, your first real partner, and your first new car (albeit a small one). You continue to burn the candle at both ends, because you now live in a bigger apartment, and you have to pay back your car loan. Regardless, you are bursting with energy (and debt!), and you tell yourself that you have your whole life ahead of you...

At the age of 30, you start to earn a little more money, and you begin looking at nicer cars, maybe your first Lexus, but, your plans change at the last minute, because you find out that you're about to have a child. As soon as you get married, (these little events are quite expensive, of course), you set out to buy your first house.

You continue to burn the candle at both ends, and even in the middle, because there are now three mouths to feed.

But you tell yourself that it's temporary, and that by the time you are forty, you will finally be able to relax, travel, and live a little.

Of course, you don't relax at the age of forty, because for the first time in your life you have found a truly interesting job, with responsibilities, but also obligations, like the obligation to work sixty hours per week!

You finally start to earn some real money, but you don't really feel like it, because you have finally purchased your first BMW, and you have a second child, which is far more expensive than the first, because you also have a second spouse: the first one divorced you because you worked sixty hours per week. You have also inherited a huge alimony payment, which unfortunately is not tax-deductible.

At the age of fifty, you begin to feel the symptoms of fatigue (which is normal when you have two children and two marriages!): you often have a sore back, you have the beginnings of a stomach ulcer, and you take glucosamine sulphate because your left knee hurts when you play golf —even when you use the cart!

You sometimes feel sharp pains in your heart, especially after your best friend suffered a heart attack, which killed him.

And you are worried, because your favourite cousin, whom you promised to see more often during your last visit to the funeral home —well, the last time you ever saw him was at the funeral home last week, after he passed away from intestinal cancer!

So you begin to understand that you are not immortal, and that now might be the time to stop burning the candle at both ends, before it's too late.

For the first time in your life, you feel as though... you no longer have your whole life ahead of you!

You finally understand that comedienne Lily Tomlin was not joking when she said: "The trouble with the rat race is that even if you win, you're still a rat."

Maybe you aren't a rat, but you are dog-tired, because you have worked like a dog for thirty years.

You may object, and tell me that there is nothing you can do about it, that everyone has the same problem, or has no time, that everyone is in a hurry, that everyone runs all the time, and that, to paraphrase Freud, it's just one of the ills of our time.

I know.

At the restaurant, at the garage, at the pharmacy, virtually everywhere you go, at every counter, you are told "It won't be long!", in order to not lose your clientele or to avoid a possible burst of rage (you are never told this at the hospital, because they know you aren't that naïve —it will be long)!

It won't be long.

You may be tempted to respond: "I hope not, because just think, I don't have my whole day ahead of me —I have important things to do!"

After you have read this little book, I sincerely hope that you will respond differently...

Perhaps you can answer like I do, because I have nothing really important to do in life, other than living it, of course!

In any case, when I am warned that: "It won't be long!" I answer: "I'm not in a hurry."

I don't say this only to be polite, but also to take some of the pressure off the employee who is serving me.

In reality, and with no exceptions, this is because I am never in a hurry. I like to take my time.

After all, it's my right —and it's my time, isn't it?

If my time is my own, isn't it only normal for me to have it and to own it, instead of allowing myself to be owned by it, like most people do?

I am often told —and I'm not sure if this is a compliment or an insult —that not only do I appear to have all the time in the world, but also I look like I'm on vacation, or just returning from vacation...

You know, that's my favourite compliment.

Let me just say that it's better to be told that than the opposite: "Hey —you really need a vacation..."especially when it's your boss who says it to you, and who decides on your behalf that it will be a very long vacation! Shouldn't we always look like we're on vacation?

That would be great, because that way, we wouldn't always be anticipating our two or three weeks of annual vacation by pitifully counting down the days and striking them off on the calendar.

Instead of looking spent, exhausted, and fed up... we could look like we've been on vacation all year long!

We'd be in a perpetual good mood!

And when the time came to take our real vacation, we would really benefit, because we wouldn't be heading into it (and coming out of it) half dead.

At the end of two or three weeks, we wouldn't feel frustrated at the prospect of returning to the office after just starting to decompress, and starting to feel our good mood returning, and that our best should be kept for ourselves, and not for our boss!

But not only do we not take frequent vacations, when we do take them, we are in an advanced state of exhaustion. That is, of course, if we do not fall sick on the first day (which is like dying during the first year of retirement!), because it's the only time our overworked body feels entitled to finally relax!

If you still don't have time, and if you still never take your time, then you are poor, it would seem. Yes, POOR, even if you have millions of dollars in your bank account, a huge house, and fancy cars.

You overlook the essential, the real beauty of life, and its true objective. In order to discover these things, and especially to be able to appreciate them, you need: time!

Time is your raw material, the substance by means of which everything is done, or undone!

It appears to me that you should spend a few hours of your life —at least one hour, at any rate: the time it takes you to read these musings —to ponder this issue.

Basically, your life depends on it. So does your health, and more importantly, your HAPPINESS.

Does anything else really matter?

With this brief and unpretentious tale, I will attempt to demonstrate to you that you can go against the grain of modern society, where progress, it would appear, has done some devastating damage.

I'll give you a few more tips —which you can add to those you already have —to enable you to free yourself, to become the master of your time instead of its slave, and to be, to put it simply, always on vacation…

In my opinion, the first step in this major undertaking is to free yourself from the tyranny of work —this is the number one vacation antidote.

✂CHAPTER 2

FREE YOURSELF FROM THE TYRANNY OF WORK!

There are two major components of your life that are responsible for devouring your time, and they have one thing in common: they are unavoidable, or at least they appear to be...

The first is sleep, to which we dedicate twenty-four years of our life, if we sleep eight hours per day!

That's assuming we live to be seventy-two...

The second is work, of course.

In general, work takes up eight hours of our day, to which we must add the hour (best-case scenario) that it takes us to get there and back...

Of course, it's often much longer, because many of you live far away, because it rained or snowed, because there was an accident, even going the other way, that caused people to slow down or stop to watch.

Sheer curiosity.

Which is dangerous, and sometimes causes another accident, only this time it's on your side, which costs you even more time!

So nine hours per day, but in reality, it is often much longer, because we often bring work (and work-related concerns) home, and we allow ourselves to be disturbed on evenings and weekends for real emergencies. Or emergencies that are invented by an obsessed boss —who lives for his job —or who is paranoid and is afraid of losing market share... or his job!

And then there is the Internet, the cell phone, the BlackBerry™, all of which makes us dogs on invisible leashes: we can be reached anywhere in the world twenty-four hours per day. What glory!

But let's say we only spend nine hours per day at work...

Yes, nine hours per day...

Five or six days per week...

113

All in all, if we really think about it, this is our biggest obligation, and we must think about it if we want to free ourselves from it!

In fact, these nine hours that you spend as a breadwinner, also represents the Minotaur that literally devours you in the labyrinth that is your life.

They represent more than twenty years of your life... (once again, if you live to be seventy-two years old).

That's nearly one-quarter of your life...

So unless you are impassioned by sleep and work, you spend approximately forty-five years of your life either doing something that you really don't want to do or simply being unconscious!

It's starting to add up, isn't it?

In any case, that's why you don't see the time passing, why you wake up one day and... you are old, very old, too old to do what you dreamed of doing while you were... less old —but now it's too late!

You put everything into your work.

Not everything, but a lot.

Far too much.

At least in my opinion.

Think about it...

Nine hours...

And not just any hours!

In general, these are the best hours of the day, the ones when we feel at our best, our most energetic...

It's a little ironic, and a little sad, to think that the best hours of your day, and the best of yourself, are being sold to a boss who often doesn't appreciate it, because he only pays you a mediocre salary!

And why should he be overflowing with recognition? It's a discount sale, a dumb sale that you agree to and trade your work for half, or one-tenth, or even one-thousandth of what you are worth!

Or rather what YOU deserve!

When you think about it, it's also a little bit sad that you subject yourself to this for so many years of your life, the years that are called the "adult years", but which should be called the "slave years", because we suddenly realize that the only time when we were free was when we were children, and we have to wait until retirement to reclaim that freedom... In fact, that could be the reason why we say that the elderly regress to childhood!

But there's a catch: it isn't even guaranteed that we'll live to retire...

And it isn't guaranteed that we'll get there in the condition we hope to arrive in…

But it is guaranteed that we'll get there in a slightly altered state, a damaged state, not quite whole…

At this highly anticipated age —anticipated for forty or fifty years —we don't always have the drive, the energy, or the health to do what we have always dreamed of doing, but were never able to do because we were obligated to… work!

And why do we accept this?

Because we are like everyone else, and everyone says that… everybody must work —that's life!

But should life "really" be like this?

Of course, if you love your job, if your job is your true passion, I'll admit that you can spend the best part of your day doing it, because in general, that's when most people are at their best…

Like the Buddhists say, we are in our dharma, or it is our mission, to use a trendy expression, which is actually a revamped centuries-old concept! I admit that we want the fun to last in that case, and therefore, we strive to delay retirement for as long as possible, because even though we are working, we are having fun…

Like a jester.

Like a wise man.

Like Warren Buffet, the second-wealthiest man in America, who at the age of seventy-four still heads Berkshire Hathaway Inc. —the company that he founded more than forty years ago —with a master's hand.

Like Li Ka-Shing, one of the richest men in Asia, who at the age of seventy-six continues to oversee the operations of Hutchison Whampoa Ltd, a huge global conglomerate.

Like Sumner Redstone, who at eighty-one is President of Viacom Inc. Like Kirk Kerkorian, who at the age of eighty-seven continues to make waves in the business world, for example by acquiring an influential position in GM by buying 7% of the stock.

Like the incredible French writer, Henri Troyat, who at the venerable age of ninety-four recently published a five hundred page biography of Alexandre Dumas!

But if you are only working to earn a living, as they say, which in itself is a strange expression…

If you cross off all the days until Friday on your calendar, or highlight your two weeks of annual vacation…

If you patiently cross off the years until your retirement…

In other words, if you would immediately submit your resignation if you were to win the million (or at least five million, if you factor in inflation!), I think you should seriously think about these nine hours…

Because these nine hours are critical, and in fact, they are the root of the problem…

You should put down your pen and seriously think about these nine hours, and attempt to see, with an open and determined mind, what you could do with them, and what I mean is how you could reduce them, not necessarily to zero, but at least considerably…

Better yet, how you could find a way to stop striking the days that separate you from your retirement off your calendar…

Because you could retire sooner than you think!

In ten years, or in just five years, by working in a way that is smarter and more profitable, by spending less, because quite often, our buying power is also the power that will send us to the poorhouse. And of course, by investing more sooner…

Yes, you absolutely must attack these nine hours per day …

Why?

Because they are holding you hostage…

Keeping you from your true self.

From your dreams…

From your wishes…

From your forgotten talents…

Because they are keeping you away and depriving you of those you love and those who love you…

But you can never see them, or see them only on the fly, and I'm not talking about your mistress or your lover, but your parents, your friends, your children…

Your children, who you see as strangers, and who are away from you five days out of seven, and who essentially grow up with strangers. We call them elementary school teachers!

Your children, who grow up without you, and as a result, whom you do not see grow up, and who often leave without even saying goodbye…

Yes, your children, those little wonders, those little treasures who you're

116

not really with, even when you're with them, because you don't have the time, because you are too busy or preoccupied, because… because "daddy has to work at home as well, and mommy has to work too, and because we have two cars and a babysitter, who are costing us an arm and a leg!"

The babysitter…

Another stranger who doesn't have the time to take care of her own children because she is obligated to look after yours in order to earn a living!

Yes, these poor children, who are left to their own devices until we ask ourselves how they turned out so badly!

Yes, these nine hours, which are in fact nine bars on your prison cell —wouldn't it be better to stop so that they can stop devouring our lives?

And maybe, in order to liberate ourselves (at least a little) from the tyranny of work, shouldn't we begin to spend our hard-earned dollars a little more wisely, and thriftily?

✄ CHAPTER 3

DON'T BUY UNTIL YOU DECIDE TO BUY

"When you finally manage to save enough to buy the car of your dreams, the one that I shot in my last campaign, I will have already made it obsolete. I am always at least three steps ahead, and I always make sure that you are frustrated. Real Glamour is the country we never find. I intoxicate you with innovation, and the beauty of innovation is that it never stays new. Another one always comes along to make the previous one obsolete. (…) In my profession, nobody wants you to be happy, because happy people are not consumers. Your suffering drives the economy. In our jargon, we call it "post-purchase disappointment".

This is an excerpt from a novel called *99 F*, a work of fiction that nonetheless contains some troubling snippets of truth, because the author, Frédéric Beigbeder, worked in a leading advertising agency for years before he became a novelist. He knows what he's talking about.

This confession by an ex-advertiser has disturbing undertones, doesn't it?

Do you have an insatiable hunger for the latest innovation?

Have you ever felt post-purchase disappointment?

One day, during the British Open in St. Andrews, Scotland, a commentator interviewed golfer Fuzzy Zoeller, a very nice man who had recently come from shopping at the lovely boutiques in the historical village. He had bought an antique, an old gold club, and the commentator congratulated him.

Zoeller lucidly admitted: "It will make me happy for five minutes!"

Isn't that something that you have often told yourself?

Or maybe you haven't had the honesty —or the lucidity —to say it to yourself?

Do you buy things (that you don't need) because you aren't happy, and because you are desperately trying to "cash in" on the five minutes of happiness that shopping gives you?

Do you buy because you are frustrated?

Because your boss or a colleague yelled at you?

Because your employee screwed up, because sales dropped, or worse — are in a free-fall?

Because your husband is ignoring you?

Maybe he lets you use his credit card because he is so busy working to pay off his debts…

Do you shower your children with gifts in an attempt to make them forget your extended absences?

Do you buy gifts that are beyond your means in order to impress those around you, your brother-in-law, your father, or to play "rich" with your friends who really are wealthy?

A lot of people shop the same way they eat.

They are ill.

Or they will become ill!

Like they say in philosophical jargon, they eat their emotions.

They try to buy satisfaction and happiness.

When we work hard, we get stressed, so we need to decompress.

And we need to be compensated.

We want fast and immediate compensation.

Fast-food happiness.

We want to reap the benefits of our work immediately.

Not next year or next month: IMMEDIATELY.

Business gurus repeat: DO IT NOW!

So that you feel like you are a man or a woman of action, and that you are capable of making a quick decision. Your motto is: BUY NOW!

Why buy tomorrow what you could buy today?

We want to feel powerful.

And the most common way for this to happen, to feel powerful, is to exercise our BUYING POWER.

But if we stop to think, isn't this really our way of helping major corporations get rich?

And even more often, in fact in 80% of cases, if we are to believe the statistics, it increases our ability to become poor and to sink into debt?

Without over-simplifying it, I think that sometimes it is worth it to realize that we are all engaged in an endless war from a very young age: it's US, with our more or less heavy piggy bank, earned with the sweat of our brow, against the ENEMY!

The enemy is a LEGION, a virtual army of soldiers, or mercenaries, to put it a better way, who all have the same mission: to get their hands on OUR dollars!

You are David!

Your enemy is Goliath, like in the Bible.

Goliath is everywhere in your life, on every street corner, in every store window, in every restaurant...

He is on every Website, leering at you from pop-ups, with his photo on every second page, and sometimes in the newspapers and magazines, unsuspectingly slipping between songs on the radio, following you to the cinema, where you go to try to forget everything: but don't forget him, he is in the advertising banners, and he slips in behind Mel Gibson and Julia Roberts as they embrace in front of a Gucci or Chanel boutique! This is called product placement (it should be called product investment!), and it generates money for the movie producers.

Goliath harasses you on the telephone, in your mailbox, and of course, on television, where you give him ammunition and make his task easier by unconsciously letting him in for three or four hours per day. But fortunately, you have the remote control, which you can use to zap him during every commercial break!

Goliath also has all the smarts of the invisible man. He is even there when you can't see him. And when you think he isn't there, he is, sneaking around, refining his ruses, and fine-tuning his plans of attack. He is everywhere. The only person who is more omnipresent is God.

That's no small potatoes!

He's George Orwell's real Big Brother.

Yes, he is everywhere, especially in YOUR THOUGHTS and your "dreams"…

He's also on the lips of your friends, your husband, your wife, your children, and your colleagues, who constantly mention him to you in all his forms, and topped with every sauce imaginable: "I've seen this, or that, or please! Daddy! Please buy it for me!"

"Yesterday, I bought myself this new gadget. It's incredible. Do you have one?"

And of course, you must hurry, like any self-respecting lemming, you must conform, or how will you look? Like nothing, or like a "minus habens", which means someone who has nothing. If you don't buy immediately, you'll look like someone who isn't in the now, someone who is obsolete…

If you want to feel important, if you want to feel wealthy, or even if you want to look like you are when you aren't, if you want to feel like you are really living, and if you want to forget that you will die one day, then there is only one cure: BUY!

Fast, and badly, and pointlessly, but buy anyway…

It will always be a matter of buying this or of buying that!

Buying in order to escape and to avoid thinking about your problems, about the void within, about the woman or man who does not love you back, about yourself, because you have never loved, maybe because the first person who should have loved you didn't; your mother, or your father: shopping is your only hope!

What Goliath wants, and what he is prepared to use all possible means to get, is YOUR DOLLARS, and he is so used to taking them from you that he feels that they are ALREADY his, even while they are still in your pocket!

In his eyes, and experience —and the majority of people give him a good reason to think this —these dollars are only in your pocket for a few days, or even hours. In short, they are in transit in your pockets before they move to his!

It isn't a level playing field. The game is lost before it even starts…
And this is true for 80% of people who lose it, who lose their shirt in their youth and spend their lives trying to catch up…

But David, despite his small size, can overcome Goliath.

He can overcome him because, as you may remember, he has a slingshot.
And with his slingshot, he has THREE STONES:

1. THE FIRST STONE is DISCRETION.

By using discretion, he sees that buying frenetically will not make him happier, and will even make him miserable and force him to work even more, and as a result, will rob him of or at least decrease his freedom, which in his eyes is one of his most valuable assets.

2. THE SECOND STONE is DISCIPLINE.

Discretion is good, but it isn't enough. Everyone knows that smoking, overeating, and drinking too much is bad, but so is too much exercise. However, very few people have the discipline to maintain a healthy lifestyle.

3. THE THIRD STONE is BALANCE

The balance that keeps us from envying the success or wealth of others, of seeing that, no matter what, we are all "poorer" than someone else. The balance that allows us to be content, that allows us to appreciate what we really have, deep down, and that allows us to acknowledge life, and not immediately become disinterested in something in favour of something else. Because that too will become uninteresting once we have obtained it!

With these three stones in hand, little David is able to defeat Goliath, and preserve or rediscover the freedom that he has lost.

If you aren't sure that you will be able to effectively use these three stones, just ask yourself the following three questions before you buy:

DO I REALLY NEED IT?

Most of the time, the answer will be "NO".

Not convinced? Try the following exercise: Think about all the money that you have spent over the past 10 or 20 years, and answer the following question honestly:

"If I asked you to trade me all of the items, articles of clothing that you have only worn once or twice, the guitar you seldom play, the circular saw that you use once or twice a year —in fact, all the items that clutter your drawers, your basement, and your garage… Yes, if I asked you to trade me all of those items for the $50,000 or $100,000 they probably cost you, what would you do?

I am almost certain that you would take the money!

I would, because now that I have all of these items, I KNOW that they are useless, and that's not because they are worn or outdated, it's because they have ALWAYS been useless!

So why not get a head start on your future, and why not, instead of buying these useless items, choose the money right away, while you still have the choice?

The second question, which emerges directly from the first, is:
"DO I REALLY NEED IT RIGHT NOW?"

Most of the time, the honest answer in this case is also "NO".

It can wait. It can always wait one week, one month, or even one year. The money will still be in your pocket, and the item will still be on the shelves, even if Goliath assures you that the super liquidation will only last 24 hours.

The third question, which is generally the most decisive question that we should always ask, but which in general we prefer not to ask, because we already know the answer, because we have been dazzled by increasingly significant credit alternatives that Goliath places at our disposal:
"DO I REALLY HAVE THE MEANS?"

If you owe money on your line of credit or your credit cards for more than one month, or in other words, if you have not been able to pay off the balance in the month you made the purchases, the answer is probably not what you want to hear, but it is quite clearly "NO".
YOU DO NOT HAVE THE MEANS!

Thinking the opposite, and acting in response to this thinking is an illusion and a trap.

I have a friend who I spoke to not only about the necessity, but even about the giddiness (of course, it's all relative) that comes from saving.

He immediately retorted: "I want to spend all of my money by the time I am dead."

That's fine.

In fact, I am sure that that if they could come back, many deceased wealthy people would be disappointed with how their heirs have spent their money.

However, the main problem with this philosophy, in my opinion, is that we generally spend our last dollar… BEFORE we die

Well before we die, in fact, and because of this, we have a problem…

So few people are balanced with their money.

Or instead, we could say that there are so few balanced people.

Barely 20% of the population, it would seem.

Most people suffer from one of the following two afflictions:

1. The most common: they spend too much, so much so that they will spend their entire lives in debt, and reach retirement age with the nasty realization that they have to tighten their belts in addition to licking their wounds.

2. Almost as common, although not as disastrous as the first, is a lack of ambition, courage, and imagination, to the extent that they do not dare to ever take a risk and invest, so much so that they vacillate instead of living to their full potential.

When it comes to your money, follow the Middle Road, like the Buddhists.

Don't buy until YOU decide to buy, and don't let others, like Goliath, decide for you, because that would mean letting them decide for your whole life.

Buy moderately, like a Buddhist.

Enjoy the things that you buy for a long time.

Because you will have cultivated contentment within yourself, which most people are lacking.

Act like a wise person…

Who does not depend on an object to bring him true happiness.

Because he has already found happiness, or at the very least is busy cultivating it, and is constantly seeking it, like he constantly strives to make others happy.

Draw your inspiration from the wise man, and from his remarkable capacity to think before buying, which is so mysterious to others, but so simple for him: he knows that his spirit, and not his possessions, is responsible for his happiness.

So why rush to buy?

He prefers to save, and to not give in to a false sense of instant gratification.

He prefers to invest in order to avoid the need to work like a slave until the end of his life: his future freedom depends on it.

And his peace of mind.

Because in reality, what is more precious than peace of mind?

And more importantly, how can we benefit from any possession, privilege, or wealth —no matter how immense —if we don't have peace of mind?

How can we maintain it when we are riddled with debt, pursued by creditors, and constantly being forced to burn the candle at both ends just to survive?

Sometimes, at Christmas, I feel a pang of sadness when I watch the circus of presents being unwrapped.

The children are overexcited as they race towards the beautifully decorated Christmas tree, they furiously unwrap their first gift, barely glance at it, and often don't even remove it from its package before quickly unwrapping the next one, which is far more interesting because it hasn't been unwrapped yet!

This is the essence of post-purchase disappointment in fast-forward.

Which, if we think about it, resembles what the children will experience once they are adults.

Except that, because they are still children, once all the presents are unwrapped, the children leave them by the wayside and go to play together. We simply return to work!

To pay for the toys (both for children and adults) that we just bought on credit!

CHAPTER 4

FREE YOURSELF FROM FALSE OBLIGATIONS
(and nearly all of them are!)

Most people are overwhelmed, living in a constant state of stress, on the verge of burnout and depression, and they feel like they are only half-alive, even though they are always burning the candle at both ends!

At the end of each day and each week, they tell themselves: "I haven't even done half of what I was supposed to do!"

I want to tell them that that's a good thing!

Yes, it's a good thing that you were only able to accomplish half of what you "had" to do, because if you had done everything, you would probably be dead, because you're already complaining that you are already half dead!

Furthermore, it's not only people with financial problems who feel the need to burn the candle at both ends. Many wealthy people I know say: "Right now, I often don't have time to go on vacation because I am too busy making money, but I'll relax later…"

It's a common illusion…

Because far too often, the time that they would have to relax never comes along, or comes along too late. It's not so easy to tour the old cities of Europe using a walker or riding in a wheelchair!

I am convinced that most people, when they get to the other side, admit that death caught them completely off-guard!

Yes, they are probably surprised, even when they don't die a violent death: they believed that they had more time!

Even people who retire are sometimes overloaded, and don't have a minute to themselves, because they have so many obligations!

Obligation is a horrible word, when you think about it, especially for someone who is retired… Obligations fill all their days, days that are numbered, because the day of the eternal journey is fast approaching...

I have a charming friend who is 70 years old, who has been retired for quite some time, and with whom I occasionally play golf.

Last time, we took his car to get to the club. Climbing into his Jaguar XJ12 —he always loved nice things! —he explained to me that he had established a very specific route from his house to the course, which allowed him to bypass three stop signs and two sets of traffic lights, thereby "saving" three minutes.

"Fascinating!" I commented politely, and forced a smile.

Quite honestly, though, I can't imagine what this retired friend could possibly want with three "saved" minutes, because in principle, all of his time is his own —not only is he retired, he is also independently wealthy... (I know, you already guessed it because I told you he drives a Jaguar)! Well, it's not so bad, I told myself, after giving it a little more thought —it's the old habit of a businessman who cannot —or does not want to —free himself from his iron collar...

Normally, it would be a pardonable crime, the inoffensive obsession of an elderly man (although young people aren't much better, are they?) wanting to "save" three minutes. But that day —horror of horrors —there was repair work being done on the traffic lanes, to the extent that it was not possible for my old friend to take his clever route. This delay sent him flying into a rage, which was definitely not the best medicine for the stomach ulcer that he had been "cultivating" for several years...

On the golf course, this friend, who was extremely tight with his time (and with that of others —this coin has two heads, and they are both scowling!) had another attack of managementitis.

Managementitis: the acute inflammation of the tendency to manage one's time —and that of others —which leads to all kinds of mood disorders, and in the end, costs you more time than it saves!

At the fifth hole (on the Bleu course at Laval-sur-le-Lac), two of my partners shot their ball into the woods that provide protection from a dogleg on the left. Only the best drivers (above-market, that is) can successfully defy it, but as everyone knows, it's a mental error that is common among golfers to believe that they can hit harder than they really can, so we often "club up", as is said in golf.

I courteously helped them to find their ball. A few minutes later, I reached my ball, which I had deftly shot to the right with a 5 wood instead of a driver because, as I neglected to mention, there was a pond on the right (certainly not an easy hole, this fifth!), so I took my time to evaluate my approach: there was a playful wind, and the green at the five is very hilly and surrounded with traps.

"We're late!" my old friend yelled to me.

I turned to look at the tee for the fifth hole, which was deserted. Laval-sur-le-Lac is a very private club, and sometimes you don't run into anyone at all for 4 or 5 holes, especially if you are playing early in the morning, before 8:00. "There's nobody on the tee," I objected.
"We're still late!" he insisted.

I had scored par on the two previous holes. And because I don't play very often, I like to take my time for every stroke, which usually means that I play better at the end of the day, because I use fewer strokes.

I didn't want to point out to him that his comments were a little un-justified, because I had helped our two partners to find their ball —a six dollar Nike ball that they believed they would be able to hit as far as Tiger Woods.

But partly to teach him a lesson, and partly because I don't like to be pushed when I am supposed to be enjoying myself and not working, I picked up my ball, gently tucked it into my bag, and said: "You're right. I'm slow. I'll go have a beer at the club while I'm waiting for you. You can mark me down as par for the remaining holes!"

My old friend understood the lesson. At least for this game, which he implored me to complete with him.

I know that there is some etiquette to golf, and that delaying the game is a faux pas.

At the club where I play, the members are asked to complete their round in less than four hours and fifteen minutes. It's somewhat of a strange rule, when you consider the fact that playing golf is supposed to be fun. It's a little strange to have to time your fun!

(I hope this benign comment will not earn me a reprimand similar to the one that was received by a member of Augusta National, who made a critical comment about a sand trap: they had it repaired, and deposited an invoice for $30,000 in his locker).

Yes, most golfers make it their mission to play their round of golf quick-ly. And it isn't unusual to hear a golfer brag about completing his round in four hours, with the same amount of pride as if he had just run the Boston

Marathon in under two hours!

Yes, there is a certain etiquette associated with golf, and very slow players are detested, but still...

It would seem that taking one's time is not acceptable.

And doing nothing, well, that's a crime against humanity!

Every minute must be used, every hour must be completely filled (with a little background noise from the TV to drown out the deafening silence that occurs between two telephone calls!), otherwise, it would be bad, and we would have to... think, and just enjoy the time passing by!

But that's just it. Time cannot just pass us by without our permission. We must control everything; otherwise it's just too painful...

But... are you like my friend the golfer?

Are you constantly on a mission?

Do you constantly seek to "save" three minutes, and do you fly into a rage that gives you ulcers if you don't succeed?

Are you afraid to slow down?

What invisible golfer is following you, forcing you to always go faster, to never take your time, and to never relax, even on the golf course, where you are supposed to be relaxed?

Do you always try to save time and go faster, even when you're on vacation?

Yes, we get caught up in our obligations.

Because doing nothing is not acceptable.

Try this experiment.

Invite a friend over and offer him or her a seat. Then do nothing, say nothing, and simply be in his or her company. Feel the discomfort that is released nearly immediately, especially if the modern "queen of the house" is not present: I am referring to the television blaring in front of your deadened spirits. "What game are you playing?" is the first question you might hear. "Is this some kind of a test?"

My six-year-old daughter often engages in this "activity" with one of her six-year-old friends...

In the morning, I drive with my wife to the street corner where our daughter catches the school bus. She runs with her friend, and sometimes sits with her on the side of a hill or a snow bank, and they sit doing nothing for ten, fifteen, or twenty seconds...

Twenty seconds is a long time for a child: it's the equivalent of fourteen minutes for an adult. What? Fourteen minutes? No, I'm joking. I was just making sure you were paying attention. Yes, adorable little girls are philosophers, without even knowing it, sitting doing nothing except smiling…

They don't even wait for the bus, too classy to waste their time with this mindless task that they have delegated to us, the reasonable parents.

Their cheeks rosy, their eyes clear as the dawn, they don't speak, they breathe the fresh air, simply happy to be together, and happy simply to be.

Yes, they take their time. They have free time. And we, who are supposed to be more intelligent than children, we who have "life experience" (what an asset!), and diplomas, are learning a lesson from them. In fact, they should be our masters of thought and in life, which comes down to the same thing. To live well, you have to think well.

I thought I would be the one to educate my six-year-old daughter, but she's the one who is educating me.

For example, barely a year ago, she took one or two "long" minutes to tie her shoes. She had discovered and perfected a method that was unique to her. It was different from the traditional method, and it was much slower. At the beginning, I would stupidly get impatient, and I would unfairly offer to help her and tie them for her, thereby depriving her of an immense pleasure, because she relished this moment of learning.

And I repeated to her the sentence that parents probably repeat the most often to their children, next to "Don't touch!", of course. This phrase is "Hurry up!"

Yes, "Hurry up", which is the deplorable mantra of parents, because it's time that is more natural, healthier, and in fact the only real time: the present.

One day, a disciple, who was exhausted, asked his spiritual master for advice.

"Run, run, run until you fall down," the master suggested.

"But," the puzzled disciple replied, "Isn't that advice a little…"

He didn't dare say stupid or strange.

The master, guessing his thoughts, added:

"It's stupid, isn't it? But it's what you're doing. It's what most people do. They run and run and run until they fall down."

Always in a hurry, people are short on time, and most of the time, they reach the end of the line without having had the time to do everything they had to do.

I even believe that most people would arrive at their own burials stressed or late if they could, only they can't! They are dead and buried —well, not quite yet, but it won't be long!

This somewhat simplistic joke reminds me of an old friend: "I warn you, it you don't come to my funeral, I won't come to yours!"

I am sure that many people have such bad habits and are so alienated that, even from the heights of heaven, they will still be acting as if their car is stuck in a traffic jam: if they could, they would unleash themselves on other motorists, on the municipality, on bad weather, and yell at the driver of the hearse: "Come on, hurry up! If I arrive late at my own funeral, what will people think? That I have poor organizational skills, and that my family doesn't know how to do things properly!"

"Relax," their guardian angel would probably say. "You're lucky. You're dead. It isn't your problem anymore. And hey! Let it be said in passing that I don't want to upset you, but most people don't even want to go to your funeral … The shorter it is, the happier they will be. If you don't believe me, just watch how quickly they leave once all the wine has been drunk at the little reception following the funeral."

So stop for a second! Not just for a second, but… for several seconds each and every day.

And during this break, do something that you should have done years ago, if of course you want to start living before you… die! And this simple thing, which has become so rare in our time, is…

✃ CHAPTER 5

WRITE: "DO NOTHING!" IN YOUR AGENDA…

The average person spends:

8 hours per day sleeping...

8 hours per day working...

3 hours per day watching television…

That's 19 hours already...

Yes, 19 out of 24 hours spent on only three activities: sleeping, working, and watching television...

That leaves only 5 short hours for everything else...

And generally speaking, what does this everything else include?

You know as well as I do, but let's take a look at it together…

There is the time we spend travelling to and from work, which is usually at least one hour, in the best case. However, if you live in the suburbs and work in the city, or if you live in a big city like Paris, Tokyo, Los Angeles, or New York, you can double this time!

There's the time we spend eating (I have included grocery shopping, meal preparation and clean-up, and travelling to and from restaurants in this), which represents two hours per day, even if we eat quickly, and badly...

That's three more hours gone!

We had already frittered away 19 hours, if you'll pardon the expression, and now we're up to 22…

So now you're left with a measly 2 hours per day for everything else: for all of your other obligations. I'm not saying that you don't draw a certain amount of pleasure from them (especially if you are a philosopher or a Zen enthusiasts, in which case I congratulate you!), but that you are… obligated to do them by definition, because they are obligations (sometimes even chores!), and they can and often do end up being annoying over the long term.

Let's review them ... calmly:

1. taking care of the house: maintenance, repairs, renovations, associated purchases such as linens and carpets...

2. answering mail (electronic and otherwise), returning telephone calls, agreeing to spend 5 minutes answering a dumb telephone survey in order to finally get rid of the interviewer who is wasting your time by explaining to him that you are busy preparing dinner, and besides, why in the world do they always call at mealtime?

3. paying bills, going to the bank, doing your accounting, spending fifteen minutes to explain to the lady from the credit card company that you didn't make such and such a purchase that appears on your monthly statement, only to spend fifteen more minutes on the telephone the next month contesting the interest that the company charged you, even though the purchase was successfully contested, doing your taxes, taking care of your investments...

4. taking care of your spouse and your (sometimes sick) children who need to be bathed; making lunches and doing homework every day; dropping off and picking up at daycare or school or at friends' houses; driving to dance class or hockey games; not to mention the dog that needs feeding and walking (a polite way of saying taking him out to do his business and then picking it up with a plastic bag, which has to be disposed of!); regularly taking the dog to the veterinarian, who will take advantage of your soft side in order to artfully relieve you of $100, which you don't have, and which you must pay on your credit card...

5. going to the doctor or the dentist for yourself, your children, or your spouse; going to the phytopherapist, or the psychologist, or the psychiatrist for yourself, your children, or your spouse, who has or is in the process of losing her mind, because she feels suffocated by her obligations, or because you live in New York City, or because you have seen too many Woody Allen movies!

6. taking care of your car (and sometimes your spouse's car), changing the oil or the tires; getting body work done because you shattered your nerves in a traffic jam and hit the brakes too late to avoid hitting the guy in front of you, who braked too fast and, late for a meeting (because you

didn't leave early enough!), or because you recklessly (if not stupidly) tried to park in a spot that was big enough for a mini Cooper when you drive a minivan, and the only thing mini about it is the name —and as a result, you scratched two sides —the side of your car and the side of the other guy's car, which was poorly parked! Because you left at the last minute, you lost half an hour writing up the report, and were late for your meeting, which then had to be postponed, and you wasted four or five hours having the bodywork done on your car, not to mention the fact that you might lose your client because he hates to wait: he is impatient and stressed like everyone else! Yikes! It's called the automobile domino effect!

7. Networking, going to the chamber of commerce, taking advancement courses for your job...

8. Taking care of family obligations (Families—I hate you!" André Gide, famous French writer) such as birthdays, baptisms, weddings, time with parents, in-laws, brothers and sisters, brothers-in-law, sisters-in-law, not to mention ex-spouses, hospital visits: in large families, this alone is practically a full-time job!

9. Shopping for clothes for the various seasons, for yourself or for the children, without forgetting the search for the missing mitten or misplaced scarf in the morning before sprinting to the school bus stop...

10. And oh, I almost forgot, last but not least, making love!

I put this… obligation —it's a strong word, but it is a conjugal duty! —at the end of the list, because this is the obligation that most established couples put off until last. It's hardly surprising, because they hate the fact that they are too tired to do it, they do it last, and as a result, rarely do it —together, that is —and end up doing it with another person, which creates other obligations: buying condoms, for example, unless of course they are complete morons and spend hours fine-tuning their alibis and their lies, buying extra "spontaneous" gifts to hide their crimes: that's the beauty of leading a double life!

Everything on this list must be completed in two hours. Yes, that's right, in two hours.

And that leaves little time for… for everything else that is supposed to be fun, exhilarating, memorable, relaxing — everything that is supposed to be the fruit, or the trophy of thousands of years of civilization: that which is so anticipated by our leisure-based society!

Yes, it leaves very little time to reap the rewards of so much effort, so much work, so many projects and courageously fulfilled obligations…

Little time to go to the cinema, the theatre, or a restaurant, café, book-store, yoga or tai chi class, or even the gym or swimming pool…

Very little time for a nice long massage, a manicure, a golf lesson to quickly cure our slice before the start of the season, or quite simply (which would be the culmination of the ultimate fantasy!) to DO NOTHING!

Yes, just DO NOTHING. Whenever you want, do it with the ultimate pleasure, while taking your time, doing it while savouring every moment, because it is a rare pleasure, even more so because it has been an eternity since you last tasted this pleasure, this privilege that belongs to children or to lazy millionaires: DO NOTHING…

And don't feel bad doing it…

Or maybe feel a little bit sorry for others, those poor souls (because in reality, that's what they are!) who don't know how, or have forgotten this joy, and who deprive themselves, through their own fault, due to their lack of originality, or gregarious spirit, or in short, because everyone around them deprives themselves, and instead behave well, or at least badly, to tell the truth, because since the age of reason, or at least since they became adults, they have allowed themselves to be overcome by their obligations, which were mostly false at the beginning, and aren't really necessary, but for some reason they have become obligations, and have ended up turning them into machines that are increasingly less effective, when it comes to… fulfilling their obligations!

Is it so surprising that these machines become increasingly depressed and worn out, and need more and more psychology, Prozac, alcohol, pot, and ecstasy (because they have never experienced true ecstasy in their lives) in order to continue to function?

No!

Because these machines are not programmed to DO NOTHING…

They don't even have the time for "sacred peace", to be able to go to the washroom without being interrupted, because yes, even what you see as being the ultimate refuge of modern solitude (how naïve you are!) does not hold up when you live with little iconoclasts called children, who don't hesitate to barge through the bathroom door while you are busy doing… what your boss does to you —to ask you to come and retrieve the ball that the younger brother has stolen from them, or to make a Nutella sandwich —and how appropriate is that?

Yes, do nothing, lounge around, sit on a bench, watch the poetic movements of the clouds, children playing, the clear water in a stream, or on a beach, the ocean, which renews itself constantly, or the graceful movements of bathing beauties!

Just taking care of… YOU!

Taking time for… YOU!

The person that you have lost sight of, and whom you would like to find again before it's too late…

Yes, your list of obligations leaves you with two hours, but the awful thing is that most people follow this terrible plan every day, without realizing that some people have two —or even three —jobs; two families, because they are divorced; and sometimes even a mistress or a lover (or both —let's get with the times!), because their official partner didn't take the time to take proper care of them!

I don't know if you're like me, but I am exhausted just reading this list of obligations!

And I know that the list isn't even exhaustive…

I'm sure you could add much more. After all, you're good at it…

So it's hardly surprising that everyone feels overwhelmed, spent, or irritable…

Of course, you'll tell me that you still have your weekends…

But by the time the weekend comes along, people are exhausted —so exhausted that all they want to do is sleep until Monday, which is exactly what they sometimes do! This is called sleep healing, and it has become a fantasy for many people!

In general, though, people cannot afford this luxury of just staying in bed for two days without being ill (it's a shame, isn't it?), because they have a whole other list of obligations, not including reviewing the file that they brought home!

Not to mention those who work all weekend, or at least on Saturday…

In fact, weekends are not generally spent relaxing or enjoying our leisure-based society, but doing everything that you did not have time for during the week, because in two hours, it's virtually impossible…

Of course, your spouse can help you, but sometimes without even wanting to, he creates additional work, simply because he leaves the toilet seat up, forgets to put the cap on the toothpaste or shampoo bottle, or clogs the drain with his long hair, because he is a huge creator of… disorder

(Because your spouse is an artist, or creative genius… deep down!")!

Yes, your spouse "creates" work for you because he borrowed your keys the evening before when he couldn't find his own, and he was too rushed to look, because he was already late —a chronic state for him, except in bed, but that's a whole other story!

And because of this, now you can't find your keys, and you ask yourself how you will get to your important meeting on time, even though you are already late… because of HIM! You quickly call him on his cell phone, which you hear ringing in the hallway, to your great joy. You hurry, thinking that he might not have left yet, but no! He simply forgot his cell phone at home!

Because you are in the hallway, you feverishly hunt through his pockets for YOUR keys. Finally, having no luck, you take a cab, and as a result, you start your day with a needless $15 expense!

Or worse yet — I have never done this, but it would appear that others have — he hasn't returned the remote control to its proper place, and you waste ten minutes (and your good mood!) searching for it, and once you find it, you realize that he didn't take the time to change the batteries, and you, yes YOU, end up changing the batteries, which are dead (like you!) because your spouse — yes HIM again - did not take the time to dispose of the old ones!

And this sends you flying into a rage, not unlike road rage, and makes you lose control, because your remote control has not been working all evening: if you don't believe me, just try watching television without it…

I have to ask myself what people did instead of watching television before television was invented. I'd love to know how people distracted themselves before 1953, not because that's when it was invented, but because it was around that year that it helped people to waste one sixth of their lives!

I guess they would have been forced to read *Stendhal's Red and Black*, listen to Bach, or spend time with their friends or their children, the poor souls!

So let's return to the couple — we always come together, and never separate for long enough to ask ourselves whom we would like to enjoy as the other half of our couple!

It is a well-known fact that being a couple takes time: it takes maintenance; you need to talk, flow, engage in psychoanalysis and therapy (as a couple, of course!):

"Darling, I'd like to talk about us!"

You've heard it before, and you know how much time it takes. You may also need to repair any cracks in the couple foundation and bridge any voids, and if infidelity or divorce are on the horizon, then you will be there for many months —good luck managing your agenda over the next few months!

Yes, you need to take the time to take care of yourselves as a couple, otherwise you risk having your relationship shrivel up and die. Like Buddha said, nothing can survive without food, and couples are not immune to this universal law.

And if we consider single mothers, who cannot rely on any help (not just financial!) from a spouse — a spouse who understands the necessity of dividing tasks equitably — it's hardly surprising that many of them are on the verge of depression, and have even contemplated suicide...

Let's get back to how we spend our time...

We have just outlined the broad strokes of your typical use of time, with the procession of obligations that go with it.

I had the urge to write "funeral procession", because most people have one foot in the grave...

Now let's get real, and carry out a useful exercise. Take a few hours of your precious time (forgo watching television for one night — just one night — is it so much to ask?) to devise a blueprint for your entire week, including your most common obligations...

Then, with this blueprint in hand, ask yourself one critical question...

❧ CHAPTER 6

ARE YOU AFRAID TO STOP?

Do you feel overwhelmed as soon as you … do nothing? As soon as you stop everything?

Like a Japanese koan asks: "What do you do when there is nothing left to do?"

Do you constantly strive, from morning to night, to feel important?

It wouldn't surprise me.

Because nine times out of ten, when we pass someone in the street whom we haven't seen for a long time, (too busy!) and we ask them "How are you?" they answer:

"It's going well —I'm working hard!"
And they say it with a broad smile, as if they had just won the Nobel Prize, or a huge lottery jackpot.

And in order to not cause them concern, or traumatize them, we answer:

"Good. I'm working hard too."

Yes, we feel important when we are busy, and one of the reasons is undoubtedly because society makes us feel that we aren't busy if we aren't running around in circles like a crazy dog.

When you do nothing, when you are alone with your thoughts, without the television, music, newspaper, or computer, are you overcome with a feeling of emptiness, or worse yet, by a feeling of unbearable existential angst?

If you work a certain number of hours, if you run constantly, is it not because you have a morbid fear (which, if it continues, may really end in morbidity) of finding yourself face to face with yourself?

Face to face with your distresses, your fears, and your complexes, which you forget when you're constantly in the heat of the action.

But if you never face your real problems, then how can you possibly hope to overcome them one day?

Are you afraid to stop?

Maybe you are afraid to take vacations, for a very basic reason:

For example, you are an executive employee at a small or large company, and you are afraid that if you are absent for too long, for instance longer than one week (don't even think about two weeks —that would be suicide!), people might start to think that you aren't indispensable, and that you are in fact "disposable", as they say, and that they can just flush you, dismiss you, and thank you on your way out.

That's it —if they realize that the firm could run for a whole week without you...

In order to make sure that this doesn't happen, you make sure you are available seven days per week, day and night, and even when you're on vacation, where your boss and your colleagues can reach you on your cell phone, by e-mail, at the cottage, on the beach —anywhere!

But in reality, work phobia is so widespread that it affects even those who are not afraid of losing their jobs.

A good friend of mine teaches at university, and in principle, has job security.

She teaches eleven hours of courses per week, has four months of vacation per year, and writes articles in order to stay visible in the intellectual community, but she works at least 65 hours per week, even though she has been teaching for ten years, and in principle, her lectures are already prepared...

In fact, this friend has less freedom than the President of the United States, and that's no exaggeration!

For example, she always turns down my invitations to play golf, while Mr. President appears to play every weekend.

In fact, she never has a minute to herself: no time to do sports, and never takes a vacation, even when her students take them —long ones at that!

Is the world upside down, or what?

What's the point of studying for fifteen or twenty years if it's only to be a slave, or to have so little freedom?

Sometimes I tell myself that this good friend (who treats herself very badly, it would seem!) doesn't believe that she deserves to have a good time or to take a vacation, and that's where the real problem lies.

Because if the President of the United States of America has the time to play golf, then in theory, everyone should have the time, because his is the most stressful and demanding job on the planet...

Are you busier than the President of the United States of America?

Are your tasks so important that you can never stop, that you never have the time to play golf or take a vacation?

And if you work so much, isn't it because, deep down, you are afraid of losing your place?

But isn't that a symptom of a deeper, ancient psychological problem, a lack of confidence in yourself and in your value, that you need to resolve before you drop from exhaustion because you are always on the front lines?

Yes, are you afraid of relaxing, and enjoying your life?

Because, for example, your father always worked hard until he got sick, and if you earn ten times, five times, or only twice as much money as him by working half as hard, you would feel uncomfortable...

Would you feel like a thief, or an impostor?

If you have an easy life, and fill your life with travel, vacations, and free time, would you feel guilty?

Are you afraid to stop?

143

✂ CHAPTER 7

TO GET THERE ON TIME, LEAVE... EARLY!
(unless you're addicted to stress!)

A few years ago, I had an agent named Guy, and he was addicted to stress.

I didn't realize it at first.

Whenever we had to take a flight to Los Angeles or New York, let's say at 11:00 in the morning, he would ask me to pick him up at 9:30.

It took thirty minutes to drive from his place to the airport.

Thirty minutes… if everything went well and if there were no traffic jams or accidents!

The airlines normally ask passengers to arrive one hour early for continental flights, which meant that we had exactly enough time… We couldn't afford even the tiniest delay...

But something always comes up, and the first problem was that my agent was never ready when I went to pick him up!

Either his suitcase wasn't packed, or he was on the telephone — a very important call, of course — and he had to make another equally important call while I waited. Nice!

At last we would leave, and I would have to speed, and go through yellow lights, dangerously overtake vehicles, and then, at the airport, I had to pray that we would find a parking space quickly, which isn't always easy during peak periods, and then hope that there was no line-up at the check-in counter, and finally, cross our fingers hoping that the customs officer wouldn't hold us up much: once your bags are checked in, the plane will wait for you, but still…

I soon realized that my agent loved this game of "beat the clock", that he was in fact addicted to stress, because it gave him the impression of being a very busy and important person!

I couldn't handle it!

The race against time was killing me, and getting on my nerves, and putting me in a bad mood, because I felt like a slave to time, when I much prefer being its master (after all, it's "my" time, and I like to take my time, as I explained earlier)!

Yes, the situation irritated me to the extent that, once I realized that my agent's tardiness was not accidental, and that it was his modus operandi when it came to travelling, I told him: "Either we leave when I say, or we meet each other at the airport…"

Case closed.

I am quite the opposite. If I have a meeting downtown at 12:00 noon, and I need an hour to get there, I give myself an hour and fifteen minutes…

I know that important people always arrive late, or at least are the last to arrive at meetings, and ask their drivers to go around the block in order to not arrive on time, to protect their image, no less, because it's important to arrive late, unless it could result in being fired…

Politicians who are overloaded do it all the time, going through life at 200 miles per hour, which ends up aging them as quickly as they renege on their promises! If you don't believe me, look at photos of them at the end of their terms, if of course they make it that far: they are transformed by power, and not for the better, and they often would not survive the stress of their jobs if not for the miracles performed by their doctors. A fascinating book has been written about this: *Ces malades qui nous gouvernent.*

I don't envy them —politicians, that is —because I want to live, and because of that, I want to age slowly!

It seems to me that nothing is worth killing my good mood, or making my heart rate go up, not to mention the fact that, at birth (according to wise men), we are allocated a specific number of heartbeats: it's up to you to use them at whatever speed you want! It's interesting to learn that we play a role in the number of years we will live!

Yes, I do my best to arrive on time, without having to run, because otherwise, I would feel like the slave, or the victim of the person who asked me to meet them.

Isn't it said, "punctuality is the politeness of kings"…?

The politeness of kings or not, what I truly hate is the race to not be late. I rush slowly, so to speak.

That's why I always try to leave early, so that I can get there early, or at least on time if something happens along the way, and something inevitably does.

Because I have noticed that, just like people always claim to be lighter than their actual weight when they are asked, people nearly always inaccurately estimate the amount of time it will take them to get to where they're going... There are even some who, even though they know they will need a minimum of one hour to get to where they are going, do not think that they are late, even though they haven't left half an hour before their appointment!

Why?

They don't know how to manage their time.

I try hard, because I know that this is one of the essential keys to happiness.

So I leave early.

If something holds me up, if I run into traffic, or an accident, I still arrive on time. And I don't get uptight! I don't enter the "road rage" state of mind, which leads to horrific murders in the United States every year.

I always ask myself how it is that, in the morning, people are so impatient and angry as soon as there is the slightest slowdown or bottleneck. If it were because they are in the process of being late for a date, I could understand it, because there's no crime worse than keeping a lady waiting, especially if she's beautiful!

But when they are in a hurry to get to the office in order to do a job... that they don't like?

Work that they even hate...

Honestly, it's beyond me.

It must be the motorist's paradox!

If we stop to think about it, these people are a little like my agent...

They aren't addicted to stress.

But they are addicts nonetheless.

Even though they would never admit it, they are addicted to the bad moods that traffic jams cause them!

Morning after morning!

Yes, it seems to me that these bottlenecks are a derivative that allows them to conveniently express their deepest frustrations, their revolt, their hatred of others, motorists or otherwise, and of the universe in general. Which, as a matter of fact, has done nothing to them, because it is simply

147

itself, and does what it can, which can't be easy, because the universe is enormous, and when it has a problem, it can't exactly be a little one! But we never hear it complaining…

I can't help thinking that these enraged motorists must not love their wives, their bosses, colleagues, clients, bank accounts, homes —their lives, essentially! —and these bottlenecks are the pretext for expressing it in a morning concert of horns, expletives, and one-finger salutes!

When they were younger, when they had neither jobs nor cars, they dreamed of the day when they would have one and the other: a job and a car. They have them now, but they have forgotten that what was once their dream is now their daily nightmare!

Of course, not everyone kills or wants to kill when they're behind the wheel, but although I'm not a doctor, I imagine that all of the levels of rage that lead up to envy or a murderous act do not exactly pump beneficial substances into our bloodstreams.

I imagine that these poisons tax (look —another tax!) our blood pressure, our heart, and our stomach, and that we might take less Prozac if we took our time more, which is absolutely free and non-taxable, at least under the current government!

A Japanese koan says: "We stand in our own shadow and wonder why it is dark."

Do you stand in your own shadow?

Are you addicted to stress?

Do you always leave at the last minute, even if you know that you will be late, and that you will be stressed along the way because (and you say it yourself) you hate being late!

But if you hate arriving late, then why do you always leave at the last minute?

Isn't it because you need this adrenaline, the same way some people need a cigarette or alcohol?

Do you have a tendency to self-destruct?

Do you subconsciously take on too much, and overload your schedule so that your stress level is always high, and practically at the maximum?

If this is true, are you aware that this stress infiltrates you like a Trojan Horse, and that soon it will cause your demise, if it hasn't already?

As for me, I take my time, and more importantly, I leave early, as a precaution that is not exactly exhilarating, but that works anyway —like many people who aren't wonderful, but who get by anyway —I don't know how they do it!

Of course I'm joking. If I was a genius, I think I would have known the answer since I first began writing!

It reminds me of a story.

One day, when I was invited to attend a conference on literacy (is that how you spell it?), a lady stood up at the microphone to tell her story. At the age of twenty, she still didn't know how to read. I told her, "If it makes you feel any better, even after writing about twenty novels, some critics have told me that I don't know how to write!"

So I leave early for my appointments.

Ahead of my schedule (any earlier and I'd be before my time!), I take an extra dose of calm, which serves as insurance for my good mood!

And that's why people say I look like I have all the time in the world. If, after having left early, I arrive fifteen minutes too early, I don't feel like a loser or an idiot, and I don't stress about it. I sometimes take the opportunity to park a little farther away and walk.

These fifteen minutes —which are delicious because they are stolen from an agenda that steals life from most people! —these fifteen minutes of impromptu walking not only allow me to stave off the portliness that creeps up on most novelists, but also allow me to air out my brain and mentally review everything that I need to discuss.

Or better yet, I give myself the right (there's no need to be generous only with others!) to loiter, to breathe in some fresh air (or whatever's left of it in the city!), and to sit on the terrace of a busy coffee shop, watch the people —a pastime, and in fact, a part of the work of any self-respecting novelist —and read the newspaper.

I also use the time to calmly return calls on my cell phone, instead of having frenetically attempted to do this before leaving, and thereby risking being late, and most certainly stressing myself out.

Which is another golden rule when it comes to managing one's time like a man who is always on vacation —you must change the order in which you accomplish your tasks.

Yes, it's quite plain and simple: change the order in which you execute your tasks.

Try an experiment, and enjoy the freedom and the calm that accompany this simple, simple task.

✂ CHAPTER 8

WHY I SHAVE IN MY CAR

I have two razors.

One at home and one in my car.

Why?

Having wisely calculated the amount of time it takes me to shave—specifically three and a half minutes and change (or rather hair!) —I determined that I would save 25 minutes per week, or 1,300 minutes per year, which represents twenty hours, by shaving in my car.

Because we are only awake for 16 hours per day on average, people (except for those with beards, and women) who shave for 50 years of their lives spend a total of sixty days shaving.

Scary, isn't it?

And that's why I usually shave in my car. If I could, I'd brush my teeth too, but I'd need a sink, and I have a feeling that it might actually be dangerous.

Those who are familiar with this somewhat strange practice think I'm crazy, or at least a little special, when in reality, I'm just a man who likes to have free time and not be in a rush!

For that same reason, I usually buy 15 or 20 bottles of mouthwash in a single outing, and only if they're on sale (even still!).

I know, it isn't really voluntary simplicity, but it simplifies my life!

And it not only allows me to save money, because full-priced Listerine is expensive (I never quite understood why — it must be a ploy to earn higher profits!).

It also allows me to save time and frustration, because I find it somewhat uninspiring to go to the pharmacy every month in order to replenish my supply of mouthwash, especially when the cashier places her "cash closed" sign on the counter immediately before it's my turn to pay, after having stood patiently in line for ten minutes!

Why does it always happen to me!

I know I might look like a harmless crazy person, or like someone who is obsessed with time...

But in reality, I am just trying to manage my time as effectively as possible, and to spend the least amount of time possible on unpleasant tasks, so that I have more left over for... pleasant activities!

My daughter Julia uses a similar trick to manage her sock drawer: it doesn't bother her in the morning to grab two socks that aren't even the same colour!

Finding her clever, I drew inspiration from her, not by wearing two differently coloured socks, but by buying several pairs that are the same colour, because I noticed, undoubtedly like most of you do, that I often wasted a lot of time —and patience! —every morning, as I tried to find matching socks, only to discover that one of them has holes in it!

Shaving in the car also has other advantages: it's a humanitarian gesture...

Here's how.

It never fails to entertain the people who are standing on street corners waiting for the bus.

When they see me working on my chin or top lip with an electric razor, they almost invariably begin to smile.

Not always, though.

One day, for example, I came close to starting a fight between a couple.

A pretty lady was waiting for the bus with her boyfriend (I assume they were boyfriend and girlfriend, because they were holding hands!).

She saw me shaving, and elbowed her friend so that he could gawk at me too: I quickly lowered my arm, and he didn't see the razor, he shrugged his shoulders, and turned around, skeptical.

I promptly started shaving again.

She elbowed him again.

He spun around, and I quickly lowered my arm. He gave his companion a look as if to say: "Are you playing with my head, or what?"

But in the end, always the gentleman, and in order to prevent the drama from escalating, I shaved for a long time, in full view of everyone! And the pretty lady smiled triumphantly: she was right once again, and he was forced to admit it.

If I stop to think about it, I'm not really that original…

In reality, I was doing nothing (once again!) but copying women! They don't shave in the car, of course, unless their names are George, but that's a whole other story…

But they put on their… make-up! They use the narrow rear-view mirror on the sun visor, and your erratic driving and overly hasty stops make them stop too, looking at you with brush in hand, with a smile that says it all!

Whatever you do, don't say anything, just smile, preferably with a guilty look on your face, even if it's about the road and not about your chaotic driving: that would be a recipe for disaster!

Yes, women discovered long before men the usefulness of taking care of their make-up in their car, and they have a good excuse: they wasted an hour choosing a dress, which should hardly be surprising, because the first thing she says to you when you ask her to accompany her to a cocktail is: "I have nothing to wear!"

So I calculated that it takes me approximately three and a half minutes to shave decently —with an electric razor!

It takes even longer with a blade, because you have to wet your face first, and then dry it after…

And sometimes, especially with a new blade —but the old one shaved poorly and you don't have all morning to get the job done, especially when… you are already late! —…yes, with a new blade it's easy to cut yourself, and you bleed, and then you have to try to stop the bleeding with a tiny but elegant corner of a Kleenex.

And later, at the office, the secretary or a colleague scratches their chin in front of you, and asks you, somewhat blatantly, what disease you are suffering from, before you realize that it's the little fleck of white Kleenex, which is now red, that triggered this humanitarian gesture…

Try this in your life, and let me know how it goes…

In any case, if I see you shaving in your car one day, I will applaud you: I'll know that you have understood me, or at least read my book!

✣ CHAPTER 9

DO YOU SPEND YOUR TIME…VACUUMING?

One day, a nice Electrolux salesman came knocking at my door.

I was 22 or 23 years old, and I was living in an apartment that I loved, even though it was quite modest and cost me only $60 per month. That should tell you a little bit about my age!

The five-room apartment in Montréal's North End was bright, large, and poetic, with its uneven hardwood floors, on which a dropped marble would have quickly rolled to the other end of the apartment, without having to make a single movement; but most importantly, this was… my first apartment! It remains in our memories like our first love, even if it was nothing to "write home about".

This young salesman —let's call him Charlie, because after all, that was his first name —showed up at the perfect time, as if he had been sent from heaven by the angel of dust, because I was waiting for a lady friend, in fact a young woman whom I wanted to be my girlfriend!

And because I spent most of my time with my books, —which I devoured and awkwardly attempted to write —my apartment seemed to be somewhat lacking in attention.

Looking very skeptical with regard to the efficiency of the vacuum whose virtues Charles had just listed. I told him: "Your appliance seems quite powerful, but can it suck up those huge dust bunnies that are nesting along my living-room wall?

"No problem."

And he demonstrated its effectiveness with great enthusiasm.

Not to spoil his pleasure by making the sale too easy, I played the same little game with the dust in my office. He deftly demonstrated again.

"Okay," I continued on to my kitchen, not half-convinced, "can your

155

vacuum cleaner make the crumbs disappear before the rodents, who are only waiting for a distraction or a moment of weakness on my part, to gobble them up?"

"But of course!"

The god who protects overworked and strung-out novelists had just made my apartment shine without me even having to lift a finger!

As soon as the demonstration was completed, I thanked the salesman and told him: "Not only are you an excellent salesman, Charles, but I am convinced that your vacuum cleaner is the best in the world!"

Enchanted, he pulled out his order book from his briefcase, and asked me my name. I stopped him.

"I have bad news for you, though. I could never buy your vacuum cleaner."

(It cost $700, which was an amount that I didn't have, and I had to find a philosophical justification for this)!

"Why?"

"Just imagine if I bought your vacuum cleaner, used it once, and died that very same day. When I got to heaven, I would feel stupid, because I would tell myself: 'The last day of my life, I did something I truly hated — vacuuming!'"

"What?" Charles protested, bowled over by this totally unexpected philosophy. "You can't think that way! You can't live your life and base your purchasing decisions on your possible death!"

"Not only can I, but I do," I explained. "Because you never know when you're going to die, and I would prefer not to run the risk, I prefer to "play it safe", and everyday I do more things that are fun and less things that are not fun."

He asked me how I earned my living.

When I said: "I'm a novelist," he replied: "Oh…", as if I had just admitted to being a lunatic, and he didn't insist. He packed up his merchandise and left.

It may seem a little excessive, or crazy, as a philosophy —I know. But that's what I think, more or less...

And I also think that too many people spend their lives... "vacuuming"!

It's a metaphor, of course, as I had to explain at a conference, to a charming lady who came to find me at the break to tell me, quite desperately: "Mr. Fisher, it took me a year to convince my husband to vacuum, and now that he's heard you, I need to know what to say to him!"

I told her what I just told you —that it was just an example, a parable. Don't get me wrong….

You are entitled to vacuum as often as you like, in the morning, in the evening, at night, especially if it turns on your wife: stranger things have happened, but if that's what it takes, run out and buy an Electrolux!

You also have the right to let your wife vacuum, if it turns her on (which I really doubt) or if it turns you on, which is possible, because you might not have the romantic talent for amorous adventure...

But —unless it is your trade, and you love it, in which case I have nothing against it —don't spend your life vacuuming.

Especially if you consider it to be an unpleasant chore, and you may be in the process of developing a genius idea for sheltering yourself from the need to do it for the rest of your life, or simply by working for a client for $150 per hour...

Don't follow in the footsteps of the common mortal, who accepts this obligation year after year, resigned out of habit to spend most of his time doing unpleasant tasks...

The ordinary man may not admit it, but his demeanour gives him away, doesn't it?

He spends his time making promises to himself, and dreaming of engaging in fun activities one day...

First of all, one day is not enough!

It should last much longer than one day — it should last weeks, months, or even years!

Secondly, he shouldn't run such a risk. He should be doing fun activities immediately, if of course he remembers how, because once he is dead, it will be too late!

Yes, he should immediately start acting like an eternal vacationer, which doesn't mean that he should forego all manual and domestic chores.

For example, I like to take care of my roses myself…

Because I love them, and consider them to be almost my children…

And I enjoy taking care of them...

I wouldn't go so far as to say that I talk to them, but I interact with them, if that's possible…

I patiently trim them, and they share their beauty, envelope me in their perfume, and present me with a puzzle or enigma when they are in poor health...

I should specify that I don't have an actual rose garden —just a few beds, and if I had 500 or 1,000 roses, like some, I believe I would entrust their care to a gardener: to each his trade…

I also take care of my vegetable garden, with the help of my daughter, which provides an education for both of us.

I often get ideas while I am doing these tasks!

It's often when I have my hands in the earth that a dazzling idea comes to me, or I find the solution to a problem that I have encountered in the novel I'm writing, a problem that vehemently resisted my intense efforts. Maybe my efforts were too intense. This is simply proof that it's better to be idle than to force an issue!

I also like to do grocery shopping, by myself or with my family. And I will never give up the pleasure of visiting the Jean-Talon Market in the summer, where I take in the sights and smells of the wonderful displays of fruit, vegetables, flowers, and fine herbs…

You see, I don't delegate everything — I'm not a maniac when it comes to domestic sub-contracting.

What I have against domestic chores is that I see so many people taking care of their lawns and gardens, driven by the fear that theirs might not be as beautiful as their neighbour's, and they furiously pull out weeds and search for the most powerful pesticides possible. In short, they spend their weekends obsessed, not only at their main homes, but also at their secondary homes. And to think that they purchased the cottage … so that they could enjoy life!

✂ CHAPTER 10

THE ULTIMATE SECRET TO MAKING
THE MOST OF YOUR TIME

Having retired at the end of his life to the library in an old castle in Bavaria that was made available to him by an aristocratic friend, Casanova wrote his famous *Memoirs*.

Impassioned by the memories of his countless romantic adventures, he noted, at the very beginning of his prodigal task: "Every day I write for twelve hours, which feels like twelve minutes!"

Twelve hours that feels like twelve minutes!

What a revealing and sublime confession!

Do the 8 or 10 or 12 hours that you spend at work feel more like 8 or 10 or 12 minutes?

Or is the opposite true?

Does every minute feel like an hour, and every day feel like a week?

Isn't it because you don't like what you do, and it's impossible to concentrate when you don't like what you do?

Isn't there a direct link between time and love and concentration?

One night, in October 1997, I had a strange dream.

In my dream, I entered a room in which I could hear several women crying…

At the end of the room was a canopy bed covered in large sheets.

I approached the bed, and asked one of the women:

"Why are you crying?"

"Because Pierre Péladeau is dead…"

When I woke up, I asked myself what the dream could possibly mean.

I had known the great businessman Pierre Péladeau for years, because my father had been his right hand man throughout his long and productive career…. And he was one of my mentors.

But to have dreamed about him?

And more particularly, of his death?

Because I was not terribly well versed in dream analysis, I put the dream out of my mind, telling myself that it was undoubtedly symbolic of the death of something within me.

I didn't realize that it was a premonition.

In fact, on December 24 of that same year, Pierre Péladeau passed away following a heart attack and a long coma.

My father, who was the executor of his will, and who often visited him during his long coma, told me one night, when he returned from the hospital: "It was strange, this evening. All of Pierre's former girlfriends were in his room, and they were crying…"

My dream came back to me.

I asked myself: "How could I have seen an event that hadn't happened yet? And if I saw it before it happened, was that not because it already existed? Because everything HAPPENS AT THE SAME TIME?"

In short, isn't it because time doesn't really exist, but is merely an illusion that fools our spirit, which is too narrow and not awake enough?

Some time after that, I had another dream.

As was often the case when I was a teenager, I woke up while I was dreaming, or at least, I dreamed that I was dreaming.

I came to a huge Greek-style temple.

A wise man was waiting for me. He was sitting in the lotus position, his face radiant, smiling gently.

He told me: "I'm living 1,000 years before Jesus…"

I wasn't sure that I understood him, and when I asked, he explained further: "Yes, I'm actually living in an era where Jesus is not born yet."

I thought about my previous dream, and this was merely further confirmation that time did not really exist, except in our spirits…

And the wise man added: "You came here so that I could tell you this:

"LIVING IN THE PRESENT MEANS LIVING IN LOVE, AND LIVING IN LOVE MEANS BECOMING GOD."